BARRON'S BOOK NOTES

CHARLES DICKENS'S

A Tale of Two Cities

BY

Polly Alison Morrice

SERIES EDITOR

Michael Spring
Editor, *Literary Cavalcade*
Scholastic Inc.

BARRON'S

BARRON'S EDUCATIONAL SERIES, INC.
Woodbury, New York / London / Toronto / Sydney

27527

ACKNOWLEDGMENTS

We would like to acknowledge the many painstaking hours of work Holly Hughes and Thomas F. Hirsch have devoted to making the *Book Notes* series a success.

All inquiries should be addressed to:
Barron's Educational Series, Inc.
113 Crossways Park Drive
Woodbury, New York 11797

Library of Congress Catalog Card No. 84-18531

International Standard Book No. 0-8120-3444-9

Library of Congress Cataloging in Publication Data
Morrice, Polly Alison.
  Charles Dickens's A tale of two cities.

  (Barron's book notes)
  Bibliography: p. 100
  Summary: A guide to reading "A Tale of Two Cities"
with a critical and appreciative mind. Includes
background on the author's life and times, sample tests,
term paper suggestions, and a reading list.
    1. Dickens, Charles, 1812–1870. Tale of two cities.
[1. Dickens, Charles, 1812–1870. Tale of two cities.
2. English literature—History and criticism] I. Title.
II. Series.
PR4571.M58   1984   823'.8   84-18531
ISBN 0-8120-3444-9 (pbk.)

CONTENTS

Advisory Board   iv

How to Use This Book   v

THE AUTHOR AND HIS TIMES   1

THE NOVEL   7

The Plot   7

    Time Sequence   12

The Characters   15

Other Elements   28

    Setting   28

    Themes   28

    Style   32

    Point of View   34

    Form and Structure 35

    Sources   36

The Story   38

A STEP BEYOND   88

Tests and Answers   88

Term Paper Ideas   98

Further Reading   100

    Critical Works 100

    Author's Other Works 102

Glossary   102

The Critics   105

ADVISORY BOARD

HOW TO USE THIS BOOK

You have to know how to approach literature in order to get the most out of it. This *Barron's Book Notes* volume follows a plan based on methods used by some of the best students to read a work of literature.

Begin with the guide's section on the author's life and times. As you read, try to form a clear picture of the author's personality, circumstances, and motives for writing the work. This background usually will make it easier for you to hear the author's tone of voice, and follow where the author is heading.

Then go over the rest of the introductory material—such sections as those on the plot, characters, setting, themes, and style of the work. Underline, or write down in your notebook, particular things to watch for, such as contrasts between characters and repeated literary devices. At this point, you may want to develop a system of symbols to use in marking your text as you read. (Of course, you should only mark up a book you own, not one that belongs to another person or a school.) Perhaps you will want to use a different letter for each character's name, a different number for each major theme of the book, a different color for each important symbol or literary device. Be prepared to mark up the pages of your book as you read. Put your marks in the margins so you can find them again easily.

Now comes the moment you've been waiting for—the time to start reading the work of literature. You may want to put aside your *Barron's Book Notes* volume until you've read the work all the way through. Or you may want to alternate, reading the *Book Notes* analysis of each section as soon as you have finished reading the corresponding part of the original. Before you move on, reread crucial passages you don't fully understand. (Don't take this guide's analysis for granted—make up your own mind as to what the work means.)

Once you've finished the whole work of literature, you may want to review it right away, so you can firm up your ideas about what it means. You may want to leaf through the book concentrating on passages you marked in reference to one character or one theme. This is also a good time to reread the *Book Notes* introductory material, which pulls together insights on specific topics.

When it comes time to prepare for a test or to write a paper, you'll already have formed ideas about the work. You'll be able to go back through it, refreshing your memory as to the author's exact words and perspective, so that you can support your opinions with evidence drawn straight from the work. Patterns will emerge, and ideas will fall into place; your essay question or term paper will almost write itself. Give yourself a dry run with one of the sample tests in the guide. These tests present both multiple-choice and essay questions. An accompanying section gives answers to the multiple-choice questions as well as suggestions for writing the essays. If you have to select a term paper topic, you may choose one from the list of suggestions in this book. This guide also provides you with a reading list, to help you when you start research for a term paper, and a selection of provocative comments by critics, to spark your thinking before you write.

THE AUTHOR AND HIS TIMES

In his lifetime Charles Dickens achieved a popularity we associate nowadays with rock stars. His works were international bestsellers, and Dickens himself was in great demand: he excelled as a speaker, an actor-director of amateur theatricals, and a dramatic reader of his own fiction. At times Dickens' skill as a public performer threatened to overshadow his writing career. It was said that women fainted by the dozens on hearing his narration of the murder scene from *Oliver Twist*. On the whole he gloried in recognition and strove to be a crowd-pleaser. He wrote novels in monthly, even weekly installments, publishing them as newspaper serials. His goal was to satisfy the tastes and expectations of a mass audience.

Playing to an audience had both a good and bad effect on Dickens' art. On the one hand his works have had wide, lasting appeal. On the other, his urge to please sometimes made him overly sentimental: once, anticipating audience demand, he even tacked on a happy ending.

What fueled Dickens' ambition? Biographers have pointed to the events of his childhood and youth, which reverberate throughout his books, including *A Tale of Two Cities*. He was fascinated by prisons, the home, the ideal woman, dual personalities, and even violence. All these concerns may be partly traced to Dickens' life; all play a role in *A Tale of Two Cities*.

Born in 1812, in Portsmouth, England, Charles Dickens was a sensitive, imaginative child. He enjoyed his schoolwork and showed promise; when a family crisis interrupted his studies he suffered an emotional trauma. Charles' father, John Dickens, was a hospitable fellow who tended to outspend his modest, government clerk's salary. After the family moved to London, John Dickens' excesses caught up with him and he was arrested for debt and sent to prison. His wife and youngest children moved into prison with him, while Charles, lodging nearby, went to work full time in a shoe-polish factory, pasting labels on bottles. He was twelve years old. The job ended within months, but Charles' memory of its humiliation never faded. As an adult he hid the incident from all but one close friend; even his wife remained in the dark.

Given Dickens' bent for concealing his own past, it's no accident that secrets and mysterious life histories lie at the heart of *A Tale of Two Cities*. The famous prisons that loom in the novel may well be by-products of young Charles' exposure to the debtors' prison. As for the blacking—or shoe-polish—factory, it must have struck the impressionable boy as his own private jail. A serious result of the experience was Charles' growing resentment of his mother, who tried, even after John Dickens' release, to keep her son on the job. "I never afterwards forgot," confided Dickens in a letter, years later. "I never shall forget, I never can forget that my mother was warm for my being sent back."

Dickens also never forgot any of his early troubles with women. As a rising young reporter in London he fell passionately in love with Maria Beadnell, a girl from a prosperous, middle-class background. Influenced by her parents, Maria rejected him. Dickens was devastated, and his enduring but limited conception of the ideal woman began to take form. In *A Tale*'s Lucie Manette you'll meet the typical Dickens heroine: young, beautiful, submissive.

A self-taught shorthand reporter, Dickens worked his way into writing for newspapers, and in the early 1830s began publishing fictional sketches about London life. In 1836 with the phenomenal success of his second book, *The Pickwick Papers*, he was free to write full time. A man of amazing energy, Dickens produced frequent novels and short stories, edited the papers in which these appeared, and commented on and dabbled in politics. In the flush of *Pickwick*'s success he married, and soon had to cope with the demands of an ever-increasing family. By the mid-1850s Dickens' wife Catherine had given him ten children—and Dickens was questioning his life's scheme.

"It was the best of times, it was the worst of times, . . ." The famous opening sentence of *A Tale of Two Cities* describes the year 1775, but Dickens might well have been characterizing his own era. Victorian England (1837–1901, the span of Queen Victoria's reign) was a society of rapid change. Dickens himself saw the coach system give way to a railrod network, and England shift from a predominantly rural to an urban, industrial society. It was the best of times for aristocrats and wealthy industrialists; it was surely the worst of times for the urban poor, slum-dwellers who labored from childhood in sooty factories. These years also saw the rise of Victorian morality, with its ideals of family life and puritan habits, even as prostitution flourished and drunkenness grew to a national epidemic.

A self-made man acutely aware of his near working-class origins, Dickens both battled prevailing trends and followed them. He was sensitive to the needs of the poor, yet delighted when he could finally afford a country house and live like an upper-middle-class gentleman. Such works as *Hard Times, David*

Copperfield, and *Oliver Twist* had satirized or railed at contemporary social abuses, making Dickens' popular reputation as a great reformer.

Yet a depression had settled on him. He was feeling more and more unsuited to Catherine. The atmosphere darkens in the novels of the 1850s: *Bleak House*, *Hard Times*, and *Little Dorrit*. Readers during these years missed the simpler pleasures and humor of *The Pickwick Papers*.

A Tale of Two Cities ran between April and November 1859 in weekly installments. It was intended both to boost sales of Dickens' new publishing venture, the journal *All the Year Round*, and as an experiment in fiction. Half the length of a usual Dickens novel, *A Tale* depends on a swiftly moving, tightly resolved plot. Dickens deliberately avoided using his trademarks of eccentric dialogue, elaborately drawn characters, and massive detail. It's important to keep in mind that *A Tale* is an historical novel, only the second one Dickens wrote. Dickens got the idea of drawing on the French Revolution as background, and took much of *A Tale*'s political philosophy from *The French Revolution*, a popular history written by his friend Thomas Carlyle (this is further discussed in this guide under Sources).

Since it is set in another era, *A Tale of Two Cities* doesn't target a specific problem of Dickens' own day. As you read look for clues to Dickens' attitude toward the common people he portrayed. Readers of *A Tale* have variously sketched Dickens as an out-and-out radical, a conservative fearful of the mob, even as a man ignorant of politics.

The novel was also influenced by Dickens' domestic troubles. In 1857, acting in a benefit performance of a play called *The Frozen Deep*, Dickens was smitten with an 18-year-old cast member, Ellen Ternan. The infatuation served to complete Dickens' break with Catherine. Several years would pass, though, before Ellen became his mistress. By coincidence, *The Frozen Deep* supplied the important renunciation theme we'll follow in *A Tale*.

Critics of the day gave mixed reviews to *A Tale of Two Cities*, but the book was very popular and holds its place as one of Dickens' best known. Reading the novel today we note the author's artistry: the concisely constructed plot, the suggestive imagery and atmosphere, the thrilling and horrifying scenes of revolutionary turmoil. For some readers the revolutionary scenes reflect Dickens' inner demons—a fascination with violence, and ambivalence toward the raging mob. But for many other readers *A Tale*'s intensity largely reflects Dickens' storytelling genius.

Dickens lived only twleve more years after finishing *A Tale of Two Cities*. His next novel, *Great Expectations*, is a return to the "Dickensian" mode—that is, it moves at a leisurely pace, boasts a gallery of complicated characters, and is concerned with contemporary social issues. *Great Expectations* is biographical, dealing with a young man's lessons in life. Yet it shares some themes with *A Tale of Two Cities;* these themes include prisons and the narrow division between reality and unreality.

In his last years Dickens was nearly the property of his public. His lifelong love of theater enticed him into giving dramatic readings of his own works. Marathon touring, including an exhausting series of performances in America, affected his already failing health. In 1870, aged 58, Dickens died suddenly of a brain hemorrhage. Though he can no longer address us from a platform, Dickens still has the power to move vast audiences.

THE NOVEL

The Plot

A Tale of Two Cities opens in the year 1775, with the narrator comparing conditions in England and France, and foreshadowing the coming French Revolution. The first action is Jarvis Lorry's night journey from London, where he serves as an agent for Tellson's Bank. The next afternoon, in a Dover inn, Lorry meets with Lucie Manette, a seventeen-year-old French orphan raised in England. Lorry tells Lucie that her father, the physician Alexandre Manette, is not dead as she's always believed. Dr. Manette has just been released from years of secret imprisonment in the Paris prison, the Bastille.

Lorry escorts Lucie across the English Channel to a house in a poor Paris suburb where her father, in a dazed state from long solitary confinement, confusedly works at the shoemaker's trade he learned in prison. Dr. Manette has been taken care of by Ernest Defarge, a former servant of the Manette family, now the keeper of a wine shop. Defarge and his wife—a strong-looking, confident woman—appear to be engaged in antigovernment activity. Lucie is saddened by her father's state and, resolving to restore him to himself, she and Lorry carry the doctor back to England.

Five years pass. In London, at Old Bailey (the courthouse) we meet Charles Darnay, a French expatriate who is on trial for treason. Lucie Manette and Jarvis

Lorry both testify that they met Darnay on their return trip across the Channel five years earlier. John Barsad, an English spy, swears that Darnay's purpose in traveling was to plot treason against England. Darnay is acquitted when his lawyer, Stryver, shatters a witness' identification by pointing at Darnay's uncanny resemblance to Sydney Carton—a brilliant but dissolute lawyer who is wasting his talents in poorly paid servitude to Stryver.

Lucie and her father—who has regained his faculties and returned to medical practice—now live happily in a quiet corner of Soho with Lucie's fiercely loyal companion, Miss Pross. They are frequently visited by Lorry (now a close family friend), Darnay, and Carton. Lucie imagines hearing "hundreds of footsteps" thundering into her life—a fantasy that in fact foreshadows the revolutionary strife in France.

The scene shifts to France. Driving in his carriage through the streets of Paris, the cruel Marquis St. Evrémonde runs over and kills a poor man's child. We learn that the Marquis is Charles Darnay's uncle (out of shame for his wicked male forebears, Darnay had changed his name from St. Evrémonde to the English-sounding Darnay). Meeting the Marquis at the St. Evrémonde château, Darnay says he will renounce the family property when he inherits to show his disgust with the aristocracy. St. Evrémonde expresses his hate of his nephew, and his continued support of the old, unjust order. The next morning the Marquis is found stabbed to death. Gaspard, the father of the boy the Marquis ran over, has killed him as an act of vengeance.

Back in England again, Darnay becomes engaged to Lucie. Sydney Carton also declares his hopeless, lasting devotion to Lucie, and vows he would give his life to save anyone dear to her.

John Barsad, now a spy for the French monarchy, tips off the Defarges in Paris to the impending marriage of Lucie and Darnay. Privately and meaningfully, Monsieur Defarge comments that he hopes destiny will keep Lucie's husband out of France.

The marriage ceremony, together with a story Darnay has told about discovering hidden papers in a prison, send Dr. Manette into amnesiac shock. For nine days, until Miss Pross and Jarvis Lorry pull him out of it, he reverts to his former shoemaking habits. We learn later that on the wedding morning, Dr. Manette secured Darnay's promise not to reveal his true name—St. Evrémonde—to anyone, not even Lucie.

Paris, 1789: the French Revolution breaks out. Defarge leads the attack on the Bastille, while his wife marshals the revolutionary women. In the country rebellious peasants burn down the St. Evrémonde château. Gabelle, the property's rent and tax collector, is eventually arrested and thrown into Paris' L'Abbaye prison. Rushing overseas, Darnay is at once seized by the revolutionaries as an aristocrat, and flung into another prison, La Force. Lucie, her young daughter, Miss Pross, and Dr. Manette rush to Darnay's aid, lodging in Paris near Jarvis Lorry, who's there on business.

As an ex-Bastille prisoner, Dr. Manette has sufficient influence to visit his son-in-law in La Force, but he is unable to free Darnay. For fifteen months Lucie stands each afternoon outside of La Force, praying that Charles may catch a glimpse of her. The Terror is in full swing, the guillotine "shaving" innocent and aristocratic heads alike.

At last Darnay is brought up before the French Tribunal. He is released through the testimony of Dr. Manette and the long-suffering Gabelle. But the very night of his freedom the Defarges and "one other" denounce Darnay. On the spot, he is hauled back to the Conciergerie, the scene of his trial. Ignorant of the disaster, Miss Pross and Jerry Cruncher, Lorry's jack-of-all-trades, go shopping for provisions and encounter Miss Pross' long-lost brother, Solomon. Cruncher recognizes Solomon as the spy-witness John Barsad who once testified against Darnay.

Suddenly Sydney Carton is on the scene (he has come to Paris to help his friends). Leading Barsad off to Tellson's headquarters for a meeting, Carton informs Jarvis Lorry that Darnay has been rearrested, and forces Barsad to cooperate with him by threatening to reveal the spy's turncoat maneuvers. Currently in the pay of the revolutionaries, Barsad's job is to spy on their prisoners, and so he has access to Darnay in the Conciergerie. Carton sets a secret plan in motion, using Barsad.

Darnay's retrial the next morning produces a sensation. A journal discovered by Defarge in Dr. Manette's old cell at the Bastille is read aloud to the Tribunal. In his journal Dr. Manette blames his arrest on two brothers of the St. Evrémonde family who had summoned him to their country house to treat a young peasant wife the younger St. Evrémonde had raped. The woman's brother lay beyond treatment, dying from a wound received when he tried to attack the rapist. After both the brother and sister had died, Dr. Manette received a visit in his home from the elder St. Evrémonde's wife and her small son, Charles Darnay. The Marquise St. Evrémonde believed the dead woman had a sister, and wished to make reparations to her. Dr. Manette attempted to reveal the St. Evrémonde brothers' infamy, but they arranged for him to be arrested and put in jail. Dr. Manette ended his story with a curse on the whole St. Evrémonde clan, and hid the document in a hole in the chimney. On this evidence Charles Darnay is condemned for his ancestors' evil deeds, and is sentenced to die in 24 hours.

After the verdict, Sydney Carton, drinking in the Defarge wine shop, overhears Madame Defarge announce that she is the missing sister, the last survivor of the family exterminated by the St. Evrémondes. She swears to complete her vengeance by wiping out all of Darnay's relations—Lucie, her little girl, and even Dr. Manette himself. Carton goes to Jarvis Lorry's lodgings where both men receive Dr. Manette, who, from the shock of Charles' condemnation has again slipped into his amnesiac-shoemaker role. Carton warns Lorry of Madame Defarge's murderous intentions, and they plan an escape from the country. Carton tells Lorry to keep the proper papers ready, and when Carton appears at two the next afternoon, all—including Lucie and her child—will ride swiftly away.

The following day, Carton enters Darnay's cell, drugs him, and exchanges clothes with him. Carton intends to take Darnay's place on the guillotine, and thus fulfill his old promise to give his life for anyone dear to Lucie. As agreed, Barsad hurries Darnay's unconscious body—dressed as Carton—out of the Conciergerie to the coach where Jarvis Lorry's party awaits. All flee successfully.

In the meantime Miss Pross, alone in the Manette apartment, has a grim meeting with Madame Defarge, who has come armed with pistol and knife to take her personal revenge. There is a struggle and the pistol fires, killing Madame Defarge and forever deafening Miss Pross. Nonetheless, she is able to meet Jerry Cruncher as they have planned, and escape.

Sydney Carton goes to the guillotine with dignity. (For the first time Madame Defarge's ringside seat is vacant.) He comforts a little seamstress, has a final vision of better times ahead, and reflects: "It is a far, far better thing that I do, than I have ever done; it is a far, far better rest that I go to than I have ever known."

TIME SEQUENCE

The series of events related in *A Tale of Two Cities* begins 18 years before the novel opens. Through flashbacks and narrations, Dickens eventually reveals these earlier events, weaving them into the ongoing action. Here is a chronological reconstruction of the complete story. Book and chapter references are given in parentheses.

December 1757   Dr. Manette is recruited by the St. Evrémonde brothers to treat a raped young woman and her wounded, dying brother. Attempting to publicize what he has witnessed, the doctor is imprisoned (III, 10).

December 1767   Dr. Manette writes a journal account of his sufferings and hides it in his Bastille cell (III, 10).

November 1775   Released to the care of Ernest Defarge, the doctor remains in a confused state. His daughter, Lucie, and the banker Jarvis Lorry carry him to London (I, 1–6).

March 1780   Charles Darnay tried and acquitted of treason at the Old Bailey court in London (II, 2–4).

July 1780   Peaceful Sunday at the Manettes' Soho residence. Lucie hears "hundreds of footsteps," signalling the approach of revolution in France (II, 6).

Summer 1780   Driving in his carriage, Charles Darnay's uncle the Marquis St. Evrémonde runs over and kills Gaspard's child. In the morning, St. Evrémonde is found dead (II, 7–9).

Summer 1781   Darnay and Stryver announce hopes of marrying Lucie. Carton swears love to her (II, 10–13). Roger Cly's funeral. Jerry Cruncher attempts to rob Cly's grave, but finds it empty (II, 14). In France the Defarges learn that Gaspard has been hanged. John Barsad appears as spy for the French monarchy (II, 15–16).

1781   Lucie and Darnay marry; Dr. Manette lapses into amnesia (II, 17–19).

1783   Birth of little Lucie (II, 21).

July 14, 1789   Storming of the Bastille; Defarge searches Dr. Manette's old cell. Start of French Revolution (II, 21).

July 1789   Peasants burn St. Evrémonde château (II, 23).

August 1792   Darnay's return to France, and imprisonment in Paris (II, 24).

September 1792   September Massacres. Lucie and her father arrive in Paris; Dr. Manette's influence protects Darnay from death at the hands of the mob (III, 2–4).

December 1793   Darnay tried and acquitted at La Conciergerie (III, 6); Darnay rearrested same night, through Defarge's influence (III, 7). John Barsad revealed as Solomon Pross, Miss Pross' missing brother; Sydney Carton exposes him as spy of the Revolutionary prisons and blackmails him into helping Carton (III, 8). Darnay's second trial; evidence from Dr. Manette's journal condemns him to die (III, 9–10). Carton takes Darnay's place in La Conciergerie; Darnay party flees France (III, 13). Madame Defarge killed; Miss Pross deafened (III, 14). Carton dies on guillotine (III, 15).

The Characters

Keep in mind that Dickens was experimenting in *A Tale of Two Cities*. He hoped to reveal character through events in the story, rather than by dialogue. He attempted to comment on French history by creating not only individuals but characters who seem to stand for entire social classes. The little mender of roads, a common man thrust into Revolutionary excesses, is one example; Monseigneur, whose chocolate-drinking requires the services of four strong men, is another.

One of the great caricaturists of his age, Dickens often found his talent hard to suppress. Remember Dickens' penchant for exaggeration when you meet Miss Pross (with her phenomenal bonnet like a Stilton cheese) and spiky-haired Jerry Cruncher. These characters may not strike you as conventionally realistic, but think again. Are they meant to be just like you and me? Some readers feel that the simpler characters, set in the framework of a dense plot, express Dickens' sense of the complexity of life.

Lucie Manette (Darnay)

One way you may approach Lucie Manette is as the central figure of the novel. Think about the many ways she affects her fellow characters. Although she is not responsible for liberating her father, Dr. Manette, from the Bastille, Lucie is the agent who restores his damaged psyche through unselfish love and devotion. She maintains a calm, restful atmosphere in their Soho lodgings, attracting suitors (Charles Darnay, Stryver, Sydney Carton) and brightening the life of family friend Jarvis Lorry.

Home is Lucie's chosen territory, where she displays her fireside virtues of tranquility, fidelity, and motherhood. It's as a symbol of home that her centrality and influence are greatest. Even her physical attributes promote domestic happiness: her blonde hair is a "golden thread" binding her father to health and sanity, weaving a fulfilling life for her eventual husband, Charles Darnay, and their daughter.

Lucie is central, too, in the sense that she's caught in several triangles—the most obvious one involving Carton and Darnay. Lucie marries Darnay (he's upcoming and handsome, the romantic lead) and exerts great influence on Carton.

A second, subtler triangle involves Lucie, her father, and Charles Darnay. The two men share an ambiguous relationship. Because Lucie loves Darnay, Dr. Manette must love him, too. Yet Darnay belongs to the St. Evrémonde family, cause of the doctor's long imprisonment, and is thus subject to his undying curse. Apart from his ancestry, Darnay poses the threat, by marrying Lucie, of replacing Dr. Manette in her affections.

At the very end of the novel you'll find Lucie caught in a third triangle—the struggle between Miss Pross and Madame Defarge. Miss Pross, fighting for Lucie, is fighting above all for love. Her triumph over Madame Defarge is a triumph over chaos and vengeance.

Let's move now from Lucie's influence on other characters to Lucie herself. Sydney Carton, who loves Lucie devotedly, labels her a "little golden doll." Carton means this ironically—he's hiding his true feelings from Stryver—but some readers have taken his words at face value. They see Lucie as a cardboard creation, and her prettiness and family devotion as general traits, fitting Dickens' notions of the ideal woman.

Readers fascinated with Dickens' life have traced Lucie's origins to Ellen Ternan, the 18-year-old actress Dickens was infatuated with while writing *A Tale*. Ellen was blonde, and she shared Lucie's habit of worriedly knitting her brows. Of course, the artist who draws on real life nearly always transforms it into something else, something original.

Finally, consider viewing Lucie allegorically—as a character acting on a level beyond the actual events of the story. Dickens frequently mentions Lucie's golden hair. The theme of light versus dark is one that runs all through *A Tale*, and Lucie's fair hair seems to ally her with the forces of light. The force of dark seems to come from Lucie's opposite in most respects, the brunette Madame Defarge.

Sydney Carton

Sydney Carton dies on the guillotine to spare Charles Darnay. How you interpret Carton's sacrifice—positively or negatively—will affect your judgment of his character, and of Dickens' entire work.

Some readers take the positive view that Carton's act is a triumph of individual love over the mob hatred of the Revolution. Carton and the seamstress he comforts meet their deaths with great dignity. In fulfilling his old promise to Lucie, Carton attains peace; those watching see "the peacefullest man's face ever beheld" at the guillotine. In a prophetic vision, the former "jackal" glimpses a better world rising out of the ashes of revolution, and long life for Lucie and her family—made possible by his sacrifice.

This argument also links Carton's death with Christian sacrifice and love. When Carton makes his decision to die, the New Testament verse beginning "I am the Resurrection and the Life" nearly becomes his theme song. The words are repeated a last time at the moment Carton dies. In what sense may we see Carton's dying in Darnay's place as Christ-like? It wipes away his sin, just as Christ's death washed clean man's accumulated sins.

For readers who choose the negative view, Carton's death seems an act of giving up. These readers point out that Stryver's jackal has little to lose. Never useful or happy, Carton has already succumbed to the depression eating away at him. In the midst of a promising youth, Carton had "followed his father to the grave"—that is, he's already dead in spirit. For such a man, physical death would seem no sacrifice, but a welcome relief.

Some readers even go so far as to claim that Carton's happy vision of the future at the novel's close is out of place with his overall gloominess. According to this interpretation, the bright prophecies of better times ahead are basically Dickens' way of copping out, of pleasing his audience with a hopeful ending.

If Sydney Carton's motives seem complicated to you, try stepping back and viewing him as a man, rather than an influence on the story. He's a complex, realistic character. We see him so clearly, working early morning hours on Stryver's business, padding between table and punch bowl in his headdress of sopping towels, that we're able to feel for him. Have you ever known someone who's thrown away his talent or potential, yet retains a spark of achievement, as well as people's sympathy? That's one way of looking at Sydney Carton.

Dickens adds an extra dimension to Carton's portrait by giving him a "double," Charles Darnay. For some readers, Carton is the more memorable half of the Carton/Darnay pair. They argue that Dickens found it easier to create a sympathetic bad character than an interesting good one. Carton's own feelings toward his lookalike waver between admiration and hostility. But see this for yourself, by noticing Carton's rudeness to Darnay after the Old Bailey trial. When Darnay has gone, Carton studies his image in a mirror, realizing that the young Frenchman is everything he might have been—and therefore a worthy object of hatred.

It's interesting that both Carton and Darnay can function in two cultures, English and French. Darnay, miserable in France, becomes a happy French teacher in England. In a kind of reversal, Carton, a lowly jackal in London, immortalizes himself in Paris.

Carton and Darnay have one further similarity—the doubles may represent separate aspects of Dickens. If we see Darnay as Dickens' light side, then Carton corresponds to an inner darkness. The unhappy lawyer is a man of prodigious intelligence gone to waste, a man who fears he'll never find happiness. These concerns mirror Dickens' own worries about the direction his career was taking in the late 1850s, and about his disintegrating marriage. It's been suggested that Dickens, though a spectacularly successful writer, had no set place in the rigid English class system. Regarded from this perspective, Dickens, like Carton, was a social outsider.

Charles Darnay

Charles Darnay has many functions: he holds a place in the story, in Dickens' scheme of history, and in Dickens' life. We can view him on the surface as *A*

Tale of Two Cities' romantic lead. We can also look for depth, starting at Darnay's name.

St. Evrémonde is Darnay's real name. He is French by birth, and English by preference, and emerges as a bicultural Everyman. He's a common, decent person, caught in circumstances beyond his control. Darnay isn't merely caught in the Revolution, he's pulled by it, as if by a magnet. He's at the mercy of fate.

Besides fate, a leading theme, Darnay illustrates a second concern of the novel: renunciation or sacrifice. He gives up his estate in France, substituting for his old privileges the very unaristocratic ideal of work. Darnay's political liberalism and decision to earn his own living (tutoring young Englishmen in French language and literature) put him in conflict with his uncle, the Marquis St. Evrémonde. If you've ever disagreed with a member of your own family, multiply your differences by ten and you'll understand the relationship between Charles Darnay and his uncle. The two men live in different philosophical worlds. Young Darnay signals the new, progressive order (though you'll see that he's never tagged a revolutionary); the older Marquis sticks to the old, wicked ways.

The resemblance between Darnay and Sydney Carton is so marked that it saves Darnay's life at two critical junctures. As we've seen, the two men are doubles. For many readers, they form halves of a whole personality. Darnay is sunny and hopeful, representing the chance for happiness in life; Carton is depressed and despairing. Both characters compete for Lucie Manette, and both enact the novel's all-important theme of resurrection. If we think of Darnay, saved twice by Carton's intervention, as the resurrectee, then Carton becomes the resurrector. (As you'll recall, Carton in fact dies imagining himself "the Resurrection and the Life.")

Many readers have noted that "Charles Dickens" and "Charles Darnay" are similar names, and they view Darnay as the bright, forward-looking side of Dickens, the hero. Though he undergoes trial and imprisonment, Darnay ultimately gets the girl and leads a long, blissful life. He has a pronounced capacity for domestic happiness, something Dickens yearned for.

There's also been debate over whether Darnay is a fully realized character or just a handsome puppet. You'll have to reach your own conclusions about Darnay, of course. In doing so, take into account that Dickens intended his plot to define character, and was working in a limited space—A Tale of Two Cities is one of his shortest novels.

Dr. Alexandre Manette

Dr. Manette's release from the Bastille after 18 years of solitary confinement sounds the first note in the theme of resurrection, and sets Dickens' plot in motion. The secret papers left in Manette's cell lead directly to A Tale's climax, Charles Darnay's sentence to die.

Does the doctor seem believable, a man of psychological depth? To support a yes answer, look at Dickens' rendering of a white-haired man, just released from his living tomb, whose face reflects "scared, blank wonder." As the story continues, Dr. Manette's spells of amnesia feel authentic. Doesn't it seem natural that Dr. Manette returns to shoemaking—the task that preserved his sanity in the Bastille—whenever he's reminded of that dark period of his life?

Less believable for some readers is the journal Dr. Manette composes in blood and haste, and hides in his cell. These readers find the doctor's journal long and melodramatic, and point to the dying peasant boy, gasping a vengeful monologue, as an instance of realism being sacrificed to drama.

From the point of view of the French Revolutionaries, Dr. Manette is a living reminder of their oppression. They revere him for his sufferings as a Bastille prisoner. During Darnay's imprisonment in Paris, Dr. Manette uses the Revolutionaries' esteem to keep his son-in-law alive. As a result, you watch him grow stronger, regaining the sense of purpose he'd lost in the Bastille.

Jarvis Lorry

All through the story Jarvis Lorry protests that he's nothing more or less than a man of business. "Feelings!" he exclaims, "I have no time for them." Mr. Lorry's time belongs to Tellson's bank, "the House," his employer for over 40 years. Yet behind his allegiance to business, Lorry hides a kind heart. When Dr. Manette responds to Lucie's marriage by falling into an amnesiac spell, Lorry deserts Tellson's for nine full days to look after his friend.

How closely does Lorry conform to modern ideas about bankers and businessmen? He admittedly values the bank above himself, an attitude you might consider old fashioned. Readers have described him as the sort of clerk Dickens saw passing in his own day, and mourned. Lorry compares favorably with the two other men of business in the story: Stryver, the pushing lawyer, and Jerry Cruncher, the "honest tradesman" who digs up bodies and sells them to medical science.

During the Revolution Tellson's in London becomes a haven for emigrant French aristocrats, the same aristocrats found guilty, a few chapters earlier, of squeezing their peasants dry. How should you view Tellson's for sheltering an oppressing class? (Dickens has already revealed that the cramped, dark bank resists change of any sort.) More to the point, how should you judge Jarvis Lorry for dedicating his life to such an establishment? Readers have suggested that Dickens, despite his liberal politics, found the solidity of institutions like Tellson's appealing; the old bank and its banker, Jarvis Lorry, represent a kind of bastion against the new, aggressive ways of men like Stryver—and against the frenzied violence of the French mob.

Madame Defarge

Dickens is famous for tagging his characters with a habit, trait, or turn of phrase. Just as Jarvis Lorry's constant catchword is "business," so Madame Defarge's defining activity is knitting. Madame knits a register of those she's marked for death, come the revolution. This hobby links her closely with the novel's theme of fate. By referring to myth, we may interpret her as one of the Fates—the Greek goddesses who first spin the thread of human life, and then cut it off. But it's not necessary to go beyond the story for other equivalents to Madame Defarge's fast-moving fingers. Dickens implicitly contrasts her ominous craft with Lucie Manette's "golden thread," or blonde hair. Lucie weaves a pattern of love and light, holding her family together, while Madame Defarge never knits a sweater, only death.

Occupying relatively little space in the novel, Madame Defarge has nonetheless been called its most memorable character. She and her husband have a curiously modern air. Perhaps you can imagine the Defarges by picturing today's guerrilla fighters in embattled underdeveloped countries. Madame Defarge is a professional who knows how to use political indoctrination. On a fieldtrip to Versailles with the little mender of roads she identifies the dressed-up nobility as "dolls and birds." She's teaching the mender of roads to recognize his future prey.

As you read, try seeing Madame Defarge as neither political force nor mythic figure, but as a human being. Her malignant sense of being wronged by the St. Evrémondes turns her almost—but not quite—into a machine of vengeance. Dickens inserts details to humanize her: she is sensitive to cold; when the spy John Barsad enters her shop, she nods with "a stern kind of coquetry"; at the very end of the book, making tracks for Lucie's apartment, she strides with "the supple freedom" of a woman who has grown up on the beach. Do you think such "personal" touches make Thérèse Defarge less terrifying, since she's so clearly human? Or does she seem more nightmarish, because, violent and vengeful, she's one of us?

Monsieur Defarge

Keeper of the wine shop in Saint Antoine, leader of the attack on the Bastille, Defarge is a man of divided loyalties. He owes allegiance to 1. Dr. Manette, his old master; 2. the ideals of the Revolution; 3. his wife, Thérèse. A strong, forceful character with natural authority, Defarge can for a time serve three masters.

There's no conflict of interest between taking in Dr. Manette after his release from the Bastille and furthering the Revolution. Defarge actually displays his confused charge to members of the *Jacquerie*—a group of radical peasants—as an object lesson in government evil.

Only when Revolutionary fervor surges out of bounds are Defarge's triple loyalties tested. He refuses to aid Charles Darnay—Dr. Manette's son-in-law—when Darnay is seized as an aristocrat; by now the orders are coming from Defarge's bloodthirsty wife. Goaded by Madame, Defarge ends by denouncing Darnay and providing the evidence (ironically, in Dr. Manette's name) needed to condemn him. Defarge stops just short of denouncing Dr. Manette and Lucie, too, but there are hints from Madame and friends that he'd better start toeing the line.

Dickens leaves us with the thought that, finally, Defarge is controlled by a force more powerful than politics, or even his wife. In Sydney Carton's last vision, Defarge and Madame Defarge perish by the guillotine. Is it fate, irony, or historic inevitability that kills them? You decide.

Miss Pross

Eccentric, mannish-looking Miss Pross is a type of character familiar to readers of Dickens' novels. Beneath her wild red hair and outrageous bonnet, she's as good as gold, a fiercely loyal servant. Dickens places Miss Pross in the plot by means of her long-lost brother. Solomon Pross is revealed to be John Barsad, Old Bailey spy and "sheep of the prisons."

Miss Pross' two defining characteristics are her devotion to Lucie and Solomon, and her stalwart British-ishness. When Madame Defarge marches in, armed, to execute Lucie and her family, Miss Pross understands the Frenchwoman's intent—but not a word she says. Miss Pross has refused to learn French.

Miss Pross' blind patriotism and devotion work to her advantage. She's empowered by love. Mistaking Miss Pross' tears of resolve for weakness, Madame Defarge moves toward a closed door, and in a heated struggle is shot by her own pistol. *A Tale of Two Cities* isn't markedly anti-France or pro-England, but Miss Pross' victory may strike you as a victory for her country, too.

Stryver

Dickens dislikes Stryver. You may be hard put to find a single lovable feature in this "shouldering" lawyer, who has been "driving and riving" ever since his school days with Sydney Carton. Yet the ambitious Stryver—his name a neat summing up of the man— is making his way in the world. With little talent for law, he pays the doomed but brilliant Carton to do his work for him. For the Stryvers of society, ambition and unscrupulousness count far more than skill. Dickens' Stryver is one of the new men of industrialized Victorian England. Abhorring his progress in real life, Dickens renders him the butt of jokes and scorn in the novel: Stryver's three adopted sons, though not of his flesh and blood, seem tainted by the mere connection.

Dickens' portrayal of Stryver as the man we love to hate seems rather one-sided. Does this make him a more memorable creation, or of limited interest? Notice how sharply Stryver is drawn in individual scenes—during his midnight work sessions with Carton, and in his conferences with Lorry about marrying Lucie. But once Lucie is married, and Darnay returns to France, Stryver drops out of the story. His role as the object of Dickens' satire is at an end.

Jerry Cruncher

For some readers, spiky-haired Jerry Cruncher supplies an element of humor in an otherwise serious novel. Other readers claim that the Cockney odd-job man who beats his wife for "flopping" (praying) isn't a particularly funny fellow. Cruncher's after hours work is digging up newly buried bodies and selling them to surgeons, which may not seem a subject for comedy. But it does contribute, in two important ways, to *A Tale*'s development.

Cruncher's grave robbing graphically illustrates the theme of resurrection: he literally raises people from the dead. (Victorian grave robbers were in fact nicknamed "resurrection men.")

One of the plot's biggest surprises hinges on Cruncher's failed attempt to unearth the body of Roger Cly, the spy who testified with John Barsad against Charles Darnay. In France, years after his graveyard expedition, Cruncher discloses that Cly's coffin contained only stones and dirt. This information enables Sydney Carton to force Barsad, Cly's partner, into a plot to save Charles Darnay's life.

As for Cruncher's moral character, a brush with Revolutionary terror reforms him. He promises to make amends for his former "honest trade" by turning undertaker, burying the dead instead of raising them. In the last, tense pages of the novel, Cruncher's vow, "never no more will I interfere with Mrs. Cruncher's flopping," finally strikes a humorous chord. It's darkly comic relief.

Other Elements

SETTING

A Tale of Two Cities takes place in England and France, largely London and Paris. The narrative starts in November 1775, but the actual events of the story begin in December 1757 with Dr. Manette's imprisonment in the Bastille. The action closes in December 1793 when Lucie Darnay and her party successfully flee France.

The historical background is the French Revolution. From page one, it approaches unstoppably. Once revolution breaks out, the action shifts to France and remains there for the duration of the novel. Which of the two cities—London or Paris—makes the stronger impression? You don't have to be familiar with Paris or its history to get a concrete sense of the city's revolutionary atmosphere. London, by contrast, may seem to fade out of the novel. With the exception of the crowd following Roger Cly's tomb, you might have trouble singling out an incident of London street life. Perhaps it's Dickens' handling of time that puts the emphasis on Paris. Book the Third covers only 15 months in a time scheme of 26 years. Yet that entire part of the novel takes place in France, mainly in strife-torn Paris. The emotion-charged events serve to make the setting memorable.

THEMES

Some of the main themes of *A Tale of Two Cities* are listed below. Notice that some themes form contrasting pairs, forces in conflict. Dickens never declares outright which force triumphs. You must decide, weighing the accumulated evidence of the story.

1. RESURRECTION

The idea of being "recalled to life" penetrates every aspect of the novel. Characters "recalled" from either a symbolic or impending death include Dr. Manette, Charles Darnay, and, in an ironic way, Roger Cly. Jerry Cruncher, "resurrection man," brings the dead back into this world in a grisly way; Lucie Manette, gently restoring her father's memory, brings the doctor back in a loving way.

In your own reading you may find Sydney Carton the most striking example of this theme. Dying in order to save Charles Darnay, Carton becomes the "Resurrection and the Life."

2. SACRIFICE (RENUNCIATION)

If we accept Carton's death as the greatest sacrifice in the novel, we can't overlook its connection with the theme of resurrection. Actually, Carton makes a double sacrifice. Long before he gave up his life, he renounced all claims to Lucie Manette. Would you consider it a great sacrifice to give up the person who might be your one chance for worldly happiness?

Other important sacrifices are made by Charles Darnay, Dr. Manette, and Miss Pross, who loses her hearing for Lucie's sake.

3. FATE

In *A Tale of Two Cities* the sweep of history and the flow of everyday life seem beyond individual control. Society's collective excesses, the greed and selfishness of the French aristocracy, bring about a revolution. As you read, be alert for correspondences between individual evil, and cruelty on a large scale. The unjust imprisonment of Dr. Manette by the St. Evrémondes leads directly to the unjust imprisonment of Charles Darnay by the people. You'll notice that aristocratic oppression both causes and resembles the Revolutionary Terror.

4. LIGHT/DARK

The world of the novel seems naturally to divide into the forces of light and dark, or good and evil. Look for golden-haired Lucie Manette to lead the forces of light. She's a radiant angel, a golden thread weaving happiness into the lives of her loved ones. Darkness and shadows have unpleasant associations with threats and death. Note the gloom surrounding prisons, hangings (Gaspard's dangling corpse casts a shadow), and Madame Defarge and company.

5. REALITY/UNREALITY

Throughout the story characters question whether they're awake or dreaming. Sometimes it's hard to decide which state is preferable. Both reality and unreality have drawbacks. The Farmer-General, a cruel oppressor, is certainly real, and the grim Paris slums are the genuine article.

For its part, unreality is the haunt of ghosts and spirits. Dickens tells us plainly that unreality pervades Monseigneur's court, symbol of the old, wicked regime. Dreams, fog, and sleep—closely related to unreality—are the conditions most like death. The doomed aristocrats Darnay meets in La Force are described as "Ghosts all!"

6. DOUBLES

The doubles you're most likely to spot at once are Charles Darnay and Sydney Carton. Yet the novel is filled with pairs: the St. Evrémonde twins; the little mender of roads/the wood sawyer; Jerry Cruncher and young Jerry.

If you contrast Darnay's generally hopeful outlook with Carton's pessimism, the two men appear to represent the light and dark aspects of life. Not all of the pairs, however, are opposites. Young Jerry seems a perfect miniature of his father, spiky hair and all.

Dickens uses repeated images of mirrors to support the theme of doubles. When you look in a mirror, you are in a sense seeing your double. For instance, watch Sydney Carton studying his own face in a mirror. The image he sees is Darnay's.

7. LOVE/HATE

Several of *A Tale*'s characters are endowed with the force of love. Observe Lucie Manette, whose "golden thread" of love symbolically encircles her family. And notice Miss Pross, aided by love in her struggle with Madame Defarge. Finally, think about the motivation for Sydney Carton's great sacrifice. In order to give up his life, he first had to love someone—Lucie—more than himself.

Love may be said to triumph in the end: Lucie and her party escape, and Sydney Carton has a vision of a better world to come. But consider the costs—Miss Pross loses her hearing, and Carton gives up his life.

Hate and its byproduct, vengeance, control the actions of Madame Defarge, The Vengeance, Jacques Three, and the faceless, slaughtering mob. To a lesser extent, Ernest Defarge also seems ruled by hate. On one hand, Carton's dying vision indicates that hate and vengeance have lost a round. On the other hand, Dickens uses his last chapter to point to the lessons of history. Crush humanity out of its natural shape, he says, and hate, evil, and violence result.

8. DEATH

Death seems to go hand in hand with resurrection. Carton has to die in order for Darnay to live. Some readers believe that Dickens displays an obsession with death. As evidence, these readers cite Dickens' vivid description of capital punishment and scenes of Revolutionary violence. These readers also single out Sydney Carton to support their argument. They suggest that Carton has a secret yearning for death and oblivion, reflecting similar feelings held by Dickens.

9. PRISONS

A looming presence in the book, prisons in England and France are linked with darkness, death, and unreality. Think about the fact that every major character either spends time in or grows familiar with a prison.

STYLE

Dickens wrote *A Tale of Two Cities* in brief, weekly installments. Not surprisingly, the limitations of time and space affected his usual style. Because the action is so compressed, and the subject matter so serious, *A Tale* contains less dialogue, humor, and detailed characterization than the typical Dickens novel. Even so, it has stylistic qualities we think of as "Dickensian," and it makes some stylistic breakthroughs.

1. USE OF DETAIL

Dickens' details have sometimes been labeled "unnecessary." Note that Miss Pross' bonnet is not only like a "Grenadier wooden measure," but like a "great Stilton cheese." Dickens also inserts extended description in the very midst of an action: recall the "gaunt pier glass" standing behind Lucie Manette in the Dover inn. One effect of these techniques is the creation of texture. After reading Dickens' descriptions, it's easy to imagine just how a person or landscape looks.

2. REPETITION/PARALLELISM

Frequent repetition of detail, dialogue, and bits of description creates a strong atmosphere. Often the repetition comes in the form of a parallel construction: remember the "best of times, worst of times" paragraph?

One way Dickens establishes character is by means of repeated traits. Nine times out of ten, Stryver is depicted "shouldering." As for Madame Defarge, her sinister style with knitting needles may change your entire conception of the hobby.

3. THEATRICAL/MELODRAMATIC QUALITY

Dickens was an avid theatergoer, and at the time of writing *A Tale* had begun giving public readings. Some of the novel's best and worst stylistic aspects—vivid imagery, heavy melodrama—reflect the fact that Dickens had performance in mind. Consider Lucie's first meeting with her father, and read the journal Dr. Manette hid in his Bastille cell. You'll notice repetitive speeches, unconvincing dialogue, and supercharged emotions. Though unlikely to show up on a modern stage, these elements show the influence of sentimental Victorian drama.

4. PATTERNS OF IMAGERY

The novel is marked by patterns of imagery that create its special atmosphere and combine with the major themes: the equation of blood with wine, the use of mirrors, and the depiction of water are among the best-developed examples. All are discussed fully in the Story section.

5.   MOTION PICTURE TECHNIQUE

Dickens' extensive use of images makes his style a visual one. If you're a movie buff, you may notice some points in common with film technique. The storming of the Bastille is described by means of rapid images, suggesting associated ideas: "flashing weapons, blazing torches, smoking wagonloads of wet straw . . . shrieks, volleys, execrations. . . . " Filmmakers call this technique *montage*.

6.   PERSONIFICATION

Throughout his story Dickens lends human qualities to inanimate objects or concepts: Hunger, Saint Antoine, and The Vengeance are a few examples. As you read, consider how personification helps illustrate moral points, and contributes to the atmosphere.

7.   LANGUAGE OF THE FRENCH PEOPLE

Writing in English, Dickens must put convincing dialogue into the mouths of native French speakers. How does he solve the problem? By literally translating French expressions and sentence structure. Depending on your tastes, the result may seem a bit stilted, or provide just the right "foreign" accent.

POINT OF VIEW

The story is told nearly entirely in the third person, by a narrator who has French history and the layout of 18th-century London at his fingertips. He tells us what each character is feeling and thinking, and shifts from the consciousness of one person to another almost at will. Technically speaking, he's an omniscient and intrusive narrator. This means he's everpresent, leading us into moral judgments about history, people, and social practices.

In a few instances the narrator takes a first-person point of view. As "I" or "we," he comments in a personal, introspective way on human nature. One result is to draw us into the fear and excitement of the Darnay party's escape from France.

FORM AND STRUCTURE

Dickens' own ideas about content, plus exterior requirements, dictated the form of his novel.

1. *A TALE* AS EXPERIMENT

Departing from his usual leisurely approach to storytelling, Dickens tries to develop character through a fast-moving plot. The actions are meant to speak louder than the dialogue. As a result, the novel is tied to its complex plot, and much space is needed simply to tell the story.

2. LONDON AND PARIS

Hoping to contrast two great cities, Dickens shifts the action between London and Paris. For many readers the Paris sections are more memorable. Perhaps, having expertly evoked London in other novels, Dickens wanted to concentrate on new territory.

3. WEEKLY INSTALLMENTS

Dickens had to publish *A Tale* in weekly serial form. He sought to attract and hold a large audience. Reflecting these requirements, nearly all of *A Tale's* chapters contain action or plot information, and end unresolved, or with a "hook." How do you react to being left dangling at the end of each chapter? Some readers enjoy being drawn in by Dickens' skillfully applied suspense. Others, while recognizing the artistry involved, may feel their emotions are being manipulated.

4. COINCIDENCE

As you read, count the number of major coincidences in the plot. Your response to the novel may depend on whether or not you can accept, for example, Ernest Defarge turning up whenever a Revolutionary leader is needed. Your hardest task may be swallowing the several coincidences that occur in III, 8. Dickens defended his use of this device. He felt, given a properly developed atmosphere, that coincidences were natural, even inevitable.

SOURCES

Two very different works were the main influences on *A Tale of Two Cities*. In his preface Dickens credits *The Frozen Deep*, a melodrama by his friend Wilkie Collins, and *The French Revolution*, a famous history by another friend, Thomas Carlyle. Drawing inspiration from others doesn't mean that Dickens copied or plagiarized. His own fertile imagination and ability to fuse ideas and select details produced an original, moving novel.

Staged by Dickens, friends, and family as an amateur theatrical, *The Frozen Deep* centers on a triangle. Two young men, both members of an arctic expedition, love the same woman; one gives up his life so the other may enjoy happiness with her. Here is the germ of Sydney Carton's renunciation of Lucie, and his final sacrifice.

At Thomas Carlyle's instructions, Dickens read through two cartloads of scholarly tomes on the French Revolution. Yet for his novel he returned again and again to Carlyle's "wonderful book." The contrast between reality and unreality owes something to Carlyle, as does the thesis of Sydney Carton's final vision: a new, better age will rise from the ashes of the old.

Among the characters with roots in Carlyle's account are Ernest Defarge, who seems to be a composite of several leaders, and Dr. Manette, who was suggested by an actual, pathetic letter discovered in a cell of the Bastille.

The Story

BOOK THE FIRST

CHAPTER 1

Here is Dickens' voice, introducing the story he's about to tell. No action or characters are presented, but the scene is set: England and France, 1775. We encounter important themes—and one of the most unforgettable opening paragraphs in English literature.

NOTE: An Instance of Parallelism

"It was the best of times, it was the worst of times. . . ," the opening words, form a good example of parallelism—the repetition, for emphasis, of a grammatical structure. Here and elsewhere Dickens relies on parallelism to balance opposing pairs, to make contrasts and comparisons. Look closely for dual themes and characters, even (in Book the Second) for dual chapter titles. Most elements in the story have, if not an equal, at least an opposing element.

With a description of a brutal punishment carried out on a French boy, Dickens leads in to two major themes: Fate and Death. Each is personified—given human identity—a trick of style Dickens will be using again and again. The "certain moveable framework" for which trees have already sprung up is the guillotine; at the moment, the sinister-sounding "tumbrils of the Revolution" are merely farm carts. The basis for their future employment, carrying the doomed through the streets of Paris, has already been laid by an unjust and ignorant society.

Dickens' tone for describing abuses is ironic, but indignant, too. Clearly, he doesn't believe that a murdering highwayman shoots "gallantly," but he does view the hangman as "ever worse than useless." Few of Dickens' contemporaries despised capital punishment as much as he did; fewer describe it so vividly. What's your reaction to the executions detailed here? Dickens himself was both fascinated and repelled by death, and generations of readers have found his attitude catching.

NOTE: Topical/Historical References

The two kings with "large jaws" and their queens, one fair, one plain, are the monarchs of England and France: George III and Charlotte Sophia; Louis XVI and Marie Antoinette, respectively.

The references to visions, spirits, and spectres mark the beginning of a deliberate pattern. Mrs. Southcott was a religious visionary; the "Cock-lane ghost" was an 18th-century poltergeist. Moving ahead to his own time, Dickens invokes the "spirits of this very year last past," meaning those spirits raised by D. D. Home, a popular Victorian medium.

These historic ghosts will give way to fictional ones. As you read, look for the mist likened to "an evil spirit" (Book I, Chapter 2), and for the "spectre" of Jarvis Lorry's nightmare (I, 3)—the image is of Dr. Manette, raised from the "death" of solitary imprisonment. References to the spirit world span the entire novel. The ghosts are here for a reason.

If you've heard many ghost stories you know that they create a weird, unreal atmosphere—exactly the effect Dickens was aiming for in *A Tale*. His spirits and spectres hint at the possibility of another world, of life beyond death. They're images that support two of the novel's themes: unreality versus reality, and—more important—resurrection.

Finally, a reference perhaps familiar from your history classes: the "congress of British subjects in America" describes the Continental Congress, which sent a petition of grievances to the British Parliament in January 1775.

CHAPTER 2

We meet Jarvis Lorry, employee of Tellson's Bank in London, traveling by mail coach from London to Dover. This is only the first of many fateful journeys—the story also ends with one. Dark, cold, and mist surround the heavy mail coach. The atmosphere is gloomy, foreshadowing more gloom to come and setting us up for the contrasting theme of dark and light.

The atmosphere among passengers, guard, and coachman matches the weather—all fear an assault by highwaymen, and so mistrust each other. Their apprehension quickens at the sudden arrival of a messenger. The messenger is Jerry Cruncher, sent from Tellson's with instructions for Lorry: "Wait at Dover for Mam'selle." Lorry's prompt reply, RECALLED TO LIFE, surprises Cruncher as much as his fellow travelers.

Left alone in thickening mist and darkness, Cruncher hoarsely exclaims that he'd be "in a Blazing bad way, if recalling to life was to come into fashion. . . !" Here is Dickens' first mention of resurrection, and first of many strong signals of Cruncher's hidden occupation. Though the action so far seems bathed in secrecy, Dickens doesn't write for the sake of confusing us. He's constantly and skillfully divulging plot, themes, and moral point of view; we have only to look out for them.

CHAPTER 3

Heading back to London, Jerry Cruncher stops at alehouses on the way, made uneasy by the night shadows and Lorry's strange message. The mail coach meanwhile bumps on to Dover, as Lorry dozes on and off through his own disturbing dreams. His present errand for Tellson's strikes him as digging someone out of a grave, and it inspires nightmare dialogues with a white-haired spectre.

"I hope you care to live?" Lorry twice asks his spectre. The answer: "I can't say."

The rising sun jolts the bank clerk awake, dispersing the night's bad dreams. Yet a seed has been planted in Jarvis Lorry's mind: being recalled to life, or resurrected, may not be an entirely blessed event. Still, the opposite of life is dismaying, as the beautiful sunlight reminds Lorry: "Eighteen years!" he cries. "To be buried alive for eighteen years!"

NOTE: A Shift in Voice

The lead paragraph of Chapter 3 is one of a very few times in the novel that Dickens changes his narrative voice. What does he gain from using "I," the first-person singular?

"I" commands attention. We note there's a break in the action, and concentrate on the meditative interjection that follows.

"I" is also a suitable persona for stepping back and commenting in general on what's been happening. Dickens as "I" philosophizes over the "wonderful fact" that human beings are basically mysteries to each other. "My friend is dead," he says, meaning, *imagine* I've lost a friend. Whether she's living or dead, her innermost personality remains secret; we can't break down the barriers of our individuality.

How does this insight relate to the story? Dickens applies it specifically to the passengers in the mail coach, all equally mysterious to each other. Yet characters throughout the novel hide secrets and memories, which even their loved ones can't decipher: Dr. Manette is one such character, Charles Darnay is another. Even Jarvis Lorry has something to reveal, as we learn in the next chapter.

CHAPTER 4

At a Dover inn, having shed his heavy overcoat, Jarvis Lorry proves to be about 60 years old. He's carefully dressed (if a little vain) and self-controlled, though his eyes hint that a lively spirit remains unquenched by long service to Tellson's.

Jarvis Lorry passes the day walking on Dover beach. It is evidently a smuggler's haunt, which adds to the air of secrecy. Lorry awaits the arrival from London of Lucie Manette, a 17-year-old orphan and ward of Tellson's. When Lucie appears, Lorry is struck by her beauty and resemblance to the child whom, 15 years earlier, he carried across the Channel on a similar errand for Tellson's. Suddenly uncomfortable, he drops a formal bow, gazing into a depressingly ornate mirror behind Lucie.

In a roundabout fashion, over protests that he is only a man of business, the bank clerk reveals Lucie's past. After her mother died, Lorry did indeed fetch little Lucie across the Channel. Now word has come that Lucie's father, Dr. Manette of Beauvais, is not dead as everyone had believed. The doctor has just been released from 18 years of secret imprisonment in the Bastille, and now remains in the care of an old servant in Paris. Lorry has been dispatched by Tellson's to identify his former client, and to escort Lucie to her father.

"I am going to see his ghost!" exclaims Lucie. Like Jarvis Lorry she imagines her father as a spectre. Unlike Lorry she responds by falling into a swoon. As you'll discover, Lucie tends to faint in moments of crisis. Dickens seems genuinely to have agreed with his Victorian readers that a proper heroine should be beautiful, good, and extremely sensitive. Perhaps you may think that Lucie could use a few coarse touches of humanity, but Dickens intends her to represent an ideal.

Miss Pross, Lucie's brawny, red-haired companion, flies to her aid. Loyalty and eccentricity are Miss Pross' two sides. We don't identify with her, but thanks to Dickens' wonderfully detailed description of her bonnet "like a Grenadier wooden measure," Miss Pross stays with us.

NOTE: A Cruel "Privilege"

Jarvis Lorry suggests that Dr. Manette was imprisoned through a compatriot's "privilege of filling up blank forms." Such forms, called *lettres de cachet* in French, were arbitrary warrants of imprisonment. Powerful French nobles supposedly could obtain them for use against enemies or offending members of their own families. In Dr. Manette's case, the fear that he was indeed jailed by noble influence, and may still be in danger, has led to Tellson's and Lorry's policy of secrecy.

CHAPTER 5

We're in Paris, at a wine shop in the poverty-stricken suburb of Saint Antoine. A large cask of wine has broken and the people rush into the street to gulp any drops they can catch. It's no riot, nothing that would make the evening news these days, but it prefigures major themes and events, including riots, that form Dickens' portrait of the French Revolution.

The spilled wine stains hands, faces, kerchiefs, and the pavement red. Its similarity to another red substance is spelled out by a tall fellow in a nightcap, a "tigerish smear" about his mouth, who dips a finger in the wine and jokingly scrawls "Blood." The joker is Gaspard, a minor character we'll meet again. He's reproached by Monsieur Defarge, the keeper of the wine shop, who asks: "Is there . . . no other place to write such words in?" In meaningful answer, Defarge places a hand on the tall man's heart. To the well-built, resolute Defarge, blood is no joke.

Try to keep the images and incidents of this chapter in mind. Now, the spilled wine turns into a harmless game, ending in drinking and dancing. Eighteen years ahead, we'll see a much less innocent dance. Saint Antoine residents will be stomping the frenzied Carmagnole, with blood instead of wine staining their hands and faces.

Pay attention, too, to Dickens' way of evoking the poverty and misery of the quarter. Today the poor are "scarecrows," clad in rags and nightcaps, but soon they'll menace the "birds, fine of song and feather"— the oppressing nobles. Again we're faced with gloom—even the lit streetlamps are "a feeble grove of dim wicks." These very lamps are destined to be used to hang men. At first glance you may find Dickens' description a bit long and repetitive, but bear with him. Not a detail is wasted; people and things (note those tools and weapons "in a flourishing condition") are brought in to build atmosphere and prepare us for what is to come.

Entering the wine shop with Defarge, we meet his wife, Madame Defarge. She is a strong-featured woman of iron composure, busy at her trademark activity, knitting. Also present are Jarvis Lorry and Lucie Manette, and three wine drinkers. The drinkers and Defarge exchange the name "Jacques," a kind of password demonstrating that they're against the existing order. Defarge directs the three men to an adjoining building. Then, after a brief conference, Defarge leads Lorry and Lucie up a dark, filthy staircase to Dr. Manette's room. Lucie trembles at meeting her father, who according to Defarge is very confused and changed.

The trio of Jacques are busily peering into Dr. Manette's room. Defarge waves them away, admitting that he shows his charge to those "whom the sight is likely to do good," that is, to fellow revolutionists. Defarge, Lorry, and Lucie step into the dark garret where a white-haired Dr. Manette stoops over a bench, absorbed in making shoes.

NOTE: A Personification

Dickens strengthens our sense of the crushing poverty of Saint Antoine by personifying "Hunger" in paragraph 6. Given lifelike attributes, Hunger "pushes," "stares," "starts," and "rattles." By the time Hunger is "shred into atomies," *we're* hungry.

We've seen personification before (Woodman Fate and Farmer Death in Chapter 1). It crops up elsewhere in this chapter—Saint Antoine is a "he"—and throughout the novel.

CHAPTER 6

Fallen into a black mist of forgetfulness, Dr. Manette can't recall his name. Like a modern political prisoner, he responds only to a number: "One Hundred and Five, North Tower," the location of his prison cell. Shoemaking provided his psychological crutch in prison, and though he's free, the doctor still pursues his trade compulsively.

Dr. Manette's emotional meeting with his daughter Lucie has drawn fire from many readers. They point to Lucie's repetitions of "weep for it, weep for it" as sheer theatrical corniness. This scene does read like a melodramatic play: father and daughter exchange speeches, father tears his hair in a frenzy, daughter rocks him on her breast "like a child." Corny by our standards? You judge. There are readers who suggest that Dickens was lifting from a highly respected source. Shakespeare staged a similar scene in *King Lear*—the reunion between the old, mad king and his faithful daughter Cordelia.

Lucie, who has inherited her mother's golden hair, looks familiar to Dr. Manette. She doesn't succeed in restoring his memory, but does introduce the light half of Dickens' light-dark theme. Lucie's an "angel," whose "radiant" hair is compared to "the light of freedom." After Defarge and Lorry leave to make traveling arrangements, she watches with her father until "a light gleamed through the chinks in the wall."

Only Madame Defarge, silently knitting, observes Lucie, Dr. Manette, and Lorry leaving Paris. It is a second night journey for Jarvis Lorry, who is reminded of his old inquiry to the spectre: "I hope you care to be recalled to life?" Lorry hears the echo of his old answer, "I can't say," and Book I ends on a note of uncertainty. Lorry wonders, and the reader wonders, too, if the doctor will ever regain his faculties.

NOTE:　　By entitling Book I "Recalled to Life," and repeating Jarvis Lorry's dialogue with the spectre, Dickens has made one issue clear: Dr. Manette, the buried man dug out alive, is a walking symbol of resurrection. This issue raises rather than resolves other points. By now you're probably asking yourself if resurrection is necessarily a good thing. Can the past be blocked out, and a person long buried truly return to life? Dickens wants us to speculate on these matters, which he explores more fully in Books II and III.

BOOK THE SECOND

CHAPTER 1

The year is 1780. Dickens gives us a view of Tellson's Bank and reintroduces the Bank's odd-job man, Jerry Cruncher, whose first appearance was on horseback, delivering a message to Jarvis Lorry.

Tellson's is small, dark, and ugly. It has always been so and, Dickens satirically suggests, its partners would disinherit their sons before renovating. A description of the bank's inconvenience and location—beside Temple Bar, where the heads of executed traitors are displayed—leads to a denunciation of the death penalty, "a recipe much in vogue."

We watch Jerry Cruncher waking up in his small apartment. Already bad humored, Cruncher catches his wife praying—or "flopping," as he calls it—and heaves a muddy boot at her. Cruncher believes Mrs. Cruncher's continual flopping is interfering with his

profits as an honest tradesman. This "trade," yet
unnamed, occupies Cruncher late at night. It has giv-
en him a permanent chest cold, and deposits iron rust
on his fingers.

Cruncher and his son, young Jerry—a spiky-haired
miniature of his father—proceed to Tellson's, where
Cruncher is at once called on to deliver a message.
Young Jerry holds down the fort, a backless chair outside the bank, wondering why his father's fingers are
always rusty.

NOTE: An Ironic Metaphor

Dickens describes Jerry Cruncher's baptism as "the
youthful occasion of his renouncing by proxy the
works of darkness." This description may stop you a
moment, since the Jerry portrayed so far seems markedly antireligious. He hounds his wife for "flopping,"
and by night engages in a secret, possibly disreputa-
ble, trade. In truth, Cruncher seems quite comfortable
with "the works of darkness," a tipoff that Dickens'
metaphor is ironic—it implies the opposite of what is
said.

CHAPTER 2

Jerry Cruncher is sent to the Old Bailey (the court)
to be on hand in case Jarvis Lorry, there attending a
trial, needs a messenger.

The morning's case is treason, a crime carrying the
awful punishment of quartering, that is, being tortured and then literally chopped into quarters. Fascinated by the almost certain doom of the defendant,
spectators jam the courtroom. Cruncher squeezes
through them in order to signal Lorry, seated among
"gentlemen in wigs"—judges and lawyers. Near

Lorry sits the prisoner's lawyer, and "one wigged gentleman who looked at the ceiling." This mysterious fellow with his studiedly casual air is Sydney Carton, who plays a decisive role in the next chapter's action.

The jailers lead in the accused, Charles Darnay. Young, handsome, gentlemanly looking, Darnay attracts all eyes; the ghoulish crowd mentally hangs, beheads, and quarters him. Darnay is charged with traveling between England and France for the purpose of informing Louis XVI ("the French Lewis") about the strength of British troops earmarked for North America. (Remember, it's 1780. The American Revolution against England is in full swing, aided by the French. If Darnay was in fact reporting British troop movements to the French, wouldn't he indeed qualify as a spy?)

Darnay faces the judge bravely, flinching only when he catches his reflection in the mirror above his head. In the midst of a nervous gesture he notices Dr. Manette and Lucie sitting on the judge's bench. His stare sets the spectators whispering about this white-haired man and lovely young lady. "Who are they?"

An answering whisper seems to contradict Lucie Manette's look of "engrossing terror and compassion." She and her father are identified as witnesses *against* the handsome prisoner.

By now you'll have noticed that Dickens ends each chapter with a hook or teaser, something to pull readers in. *A Tale of Two Cities* was published in weekly installments, and Dickens' sales depended on his ability to sustain suspense.

At the end of this chapter, when the prosecutor rises to "hammer the nails into the scaffold," we realize that it's Charles Darnay's scaffold. Most readers, both fearing and fascinated by the prospect of death, will keep turning the pages.

CHAPTER 3

The account of Charles Darnay's trial is written in several styles, reflecting Dickens' attitude toward each character and toward legal proceedings in general. A one-time law clerk, he loved to deflate puffed-up terminology and traditions.

The opening speech made by the Attorney-General (the prosecutor) is pompous and long winded, typically bureaucratic. According to the Attorney-General, his two leading witnesses are men of shining character and patriotism. Are we to believe this? The Attorney-General's exaggerated tone tells us to take his speech with a grain of salt.

John Barsad, the first witness, is called. He releases "his noble bosom of its burden" but can't escape a cross-examination from Darnay's lawyer. Dickens' masterly use of satire raises serious doubts about the nobility of Barsad's bosom. A few sharp questions from Darnay's lawyer (soon introduced as Stryver) do the trick.

Barsad soon emerges as a debtor and card cheat who has forced his friendship on Charles Darnay. Though he vigorously denies it, Barsad appears to be a government spy, paid to entrap others. Given Dickens' unfavorable portrait of Barsad, how do you think the author felt about government spying?

Stryver also damages the credibility of Roger Cly, the state's second witness. Cly, Darnay's servant, is shown to be a thief and a pal of Barsad. Stryver suggests that the two men conspired to plant incriminating papers on the defendant.

Next on the witness stand is Jarvis Lorry, who admits to meeting Darnay in November 1775 on a packet-ship returning from France. On board with Lorry were Dr. Manette and Lucie, who are both called as witnesses.

Lucie's testimony betrays her affection for Charles Darnay but doesn't help his cause. She reveals that he was traveling under an assumed name, and engaged in "delicate" business with two Frenchmen who got off the ship before it left shore.

As for Dr. Manette, he remembers nothing of the journey. We see him now as a vigorous man, restored to his faculties. Yet the doctor's mind remains blank from the time he was making shoes in prison to the moment he recovered and found himself living in London.

A "singular circumstance" arises as the state tries to prove that Charles Darnay rode in the same mail coach as Jarvis Lorry, sharing the journey that opened the novel. The state claims that Darnay disembarked before Dover and backtracked to a military garrison to gather information on the British army. Just as a witness identifies Darnay as the right man, a note passes between the seemingly nonchalant Carton and Stryver, shivering this part of the case "to useless timber." Carton has noticed that he and Darnay are doubles, almost perfect look-alikes. Faced with two such similar men in the same courtroom, the witness can't make a positive identification.

In his final argument Stryver again emphasizes how Darnay was framed by Barsad and Cly. The lawyer points out that Darnay often crosses to France on family matters he can't disclose. Notice the skillful way that Dickens, while unraveling the mystery of

Charles Darnay's imprisonment, spins yet another thread of suspense. What are Darnay's family matters? Why is he forbidden "even for his life" to reveal them? In a novel as meticulously plotted as this one, you can look forward to learning the secret of Darnay's family.

The Attorney-General finishes his closing argument and the jury begins deliberations. Sydney Carton gazes carelessly at the ceiling, but, somehow, the sight of Lucie Manette fainting doesn't escape him. He orders an officer to carry her out, and assures Darnay, awaiting his verdict in the prisoners' dock, that Lucie feels better. This first encounter between Carton and Darnay, men so alike they could be twins, isn't exactly brotherly. What do you make of Carton's manner, "so careless as to be almost insolent"? On the one hand, Carton looks so disrespectable that even Jerry Cruncher—who's no gentleman—distrusts him. On the other hand, Carton's quick action at spotting the mutual likeness and alerting Stryver has just ruined the strongest part of the state's case. Carton is a man of contrasts, well-suited to a story of contrasts; you'll have many more opportunities to judge his character.

The verdict comes back: acquitted! Lorry scrawls the single word on a piece of paper and hands it, for swift delivery, to Jerry Cruncher.

"If you had sent the message, 'Recalled to life,' again," mutters Cruncher, "I should have known what you meant, this time." Cruncher's response ties Charles Darnay into the theme of resurrection, first stated by Dr. Manette's release from the Bastille. Darnay, too, has been "recalled to life," largely through the agency of Sydney Carton.

CHAPTER 4

Dr. Manette, Lucie, Stryver, and Lorry gather around to congratulate Charles Darnay, giving us a closeup view of characters only glimpsed in the courtroom. Dr. Manette, though "intellectual" and "upright," still displays symptoms of his prison ordeal. Only Lucie can charm away his dark moods. Dickens likens her to a "golden thread" uniting her father to the time before and after his misery. Indeed, "The Golden Thread" title of Book II signifies tranquility and domestic peace. It soothes Dr. Manette's "black brooding," and yet, as Book II progresses, will be threatened by other dark forces. As the story continues, watch for explicit contrasts between light and dark.

A swift, on-target sketch of the lawyer Stryver—he's "stout, loud, red, bluff, and free from any drawback of delicacy"—is followed by an uncomfortable exchange between Lorry and Carton. The heart of the chapter, though, is the second meeting between the doubles.

NOTE:
You can read Carton's evident hostility toward Darnay as jealousy, self-pity, drunkenness, or a combination of the three. Yet keep in mind that no one but Stryver knows of Carton's role in saving Darnay's life; Carton himself doesn't mention it. Carton's actions, good and bad, ultimately lead to his great sacrifice at the end of the novel. You'll be constantly reevaluating your feelings toward Carton. He's an outsider, a drunk, a man who pities himself, yet he has a firm grip on our sympathy.

When Darnay leaves him, Carton, half-drunk, goes to a mirror and studies his reflection. This is the third time Dickens has lingered on a mirror. One hung in the courtroom above Charles Darnay, another stood behind Lucie Manette at the Dover inn. Mirrors have multiple meanings in *A Tale;* they may express unreality, self-division, ghosts, the past, death, and dreams. (The mirror above Darnay in the Old Bailey had stored up reflections of "crowds of the wicked and the wretched," all of them dead.)

On one level, the mirror Carton stares into, distractedly, shows his close resemblance to Darnay. The two men are such "mirror images" that Darnay, previously left alone with his "double of coarse deportment," felt himself in a dream. Yet the mirror also shows Carton what he might have been, and occasionally is: a man like Darnay. In this way it expresses Carton's sense of the two different sides of his nature.

CHAPTER 5

We zero in on the relationship between Stryver and Carton, learning that the apparently lazy Carton is the secret behind Stryver's legal success. It is Carton the "jackal" who extracts the essence from stacks of legal documents and prepares it for Stryver.

What motivates Carton to do another man's hack work, to serve as his jackal? At this point our only answer is that Carton has always been this way. Have you known students who do homework for others while neglecting their own assignments? This has been Carton's practice ever since he was a schoolboy.

Darnay's release is a triumph for Stryver. Carton, however, responds with such gloom that Stryver remarks on it, and then offers a toast to Lucie Manette, "the pretty witness."

"A golden-haired doll," answers Carton. This may remind you of a small boy trying to deny a crush. Some readers have latched on to the words "golden-haired doll" as a telling assessment of Lucie's personality. Do you think Carton really means what he says—or, as Stryver hints, is he only trying to conceal his dawning interest in Lucie?

The chapter ends with Carton descending from Stryver's lodgings into a cold, overcast dawn. For a moment the jackal sees "a mirage of honourable ambition, self-denial, and perseverance." But the vision evaporates, and once home Carton rests his head on a pillow "wet with wasted tears." Our impression of Carton is evolving, from a ne'er-do-well to a struggling man: unsure, unhappy, divided against himself.

CHAPTER 6

This chapter sets up a contrast between domestic tranquility and impending fate. Dickens' notion of the ideal home is here represented by the Manette's quiet corner house in Soho. Lucie has enlivened her surroundings with a French flair for interior decoration and skill at attracting company. Frequent visitors include Jarvis Lorry, now a faithful family friend; Sydney Carton; and Charles Darnay, who was released four months ago. The ideal home is also represented by Miss Pross, Lucie's eccentric, devoted servant. Steadfastly British (at the end of Chapter 3 she refused

to cross the Channel), Miss Pross' only visible flaw is
an unstinting loyalty to her black-sheep brother, Solomon. He has speculated away all his sister's money,
and vanished.

But fate—a force larger than life—intrudes into the
place that Lucie and her father have carved out for
themselves.

The chapter title "Hundreds of People" refers on
one level to echoes from the street adjoining the
Manettes' house. "Hundreds" is also Miss Pross' esti-
mate—a jealous exaggeration—of the many visitors
for her "Ladybird," Lucie. For Lucie herself, the echoes from the street are ominous, heralds of "all the
footsteps that are coming by-and-by into our lives."

The thunder and lightning of the late-night storm
strike a menacing note into the peaceful Sunday gathering of the Manettes, Lorry, Darnay, and Carton.

Charles Darnay's reference to a message written by
a prisoner in the Tower of London, and later found
crumbled to dust, turns Dr. Manette pale. We know
that the doctor keeps his shoemaking tools handy in
his bedroom—their presence signifies how easily his
mind can slip back into "its old prison," the past.

The closing paragraph is obvious foreshadowing.
The next chapter shifts us to France, giving an idea of
where the "great crowd of people with its rush and
roar," will come from.

CHAPTER 7

The key words in this chapter, which takes us
across the Channel, are "reality" and "unreality."

Unreality is the note pervading the reception of
Monseigneur, "one of the great lords in power at the
Court." Monseigneur's rooms are gorgeous, but "not
a sound business" when compared with the nearby

slums. Monseigneur's guests consist of ignorant military officers, loose-living priests, and Unbelieving Philosophers. In short, they're fakes, people of high position but few credentials.

The most solid citizen in attendance, the person who does exactly what his title announces, is the Farmer-General. He has bought the right to collect taxes for Monseigneur, a position granting unlimited license to steal from the peasantry. Historians consider the Farmer-General system one of the abuses that helped cause the French Revolution; it makes sense that Dickens, laying groundwork for the strife to come, mentions it.

Can you list Monseigneur's character traits? For many readers, such individual traits are missing. They find Monseigneur the personification of an entire class, a symbol for the ruling nobility. Thinking along the same lines, other readers believe that Monsieur the Marquis, introduced as he leaves Monseigneur's rooms in disfavor, personifies the French rural gentry. Let's check this interpretation of the Marquis against his actual behavior.

The Marquis orders his coach driven recklessly through the streets of Paris, an abuse of power consistent with his social position. A child is run over and killed, and, with typically aristocratic scorn, the Marquis tosses a gold coin to the grieving father. He is Gaspard, the tall man we last saw smearing the word BLOOD on a Saint Antoine wall.

When Defarge offers practical consolation to Gaspard, the Marquis tosses Defarge a second coin, which is at once tossed back. "You dogs!" says the Marquis, assuring the crowd that he'd like nothing better than to crush the thrower of the coin beneath his coach wheels.

Now, consider. Does the Marquis' extra bit of callousness strike you as one more mark of the privileged classes? Or does he emerge as an individual, if cruel, personality?

NOTE: The Fountain Runs Its Course

Gaspard's baby is killed near the communal fountain of Saint Antoine. In the upcoming chapter two more fountains flow—one in the Marquis' village, and the other at his country house. Dickens' use of water imagery follows a pattern. The Saint Antoine and village fountains are, first of all, centers of neighborhood activity and sources of life-sustaining water. But, already, the Saint Antoine fountain suggests fate: "The water of the fountain ran, the swift river ran, . . . all things ran their course."

Later the water swells into a sea (II, 22) and metamorphoses into fire (II, 23). Flood and fire, both natural disasters, become apt metaphors for the raging destructiveness of the Revolutionary mobs.

CHAPTER 8

This "Monseigneur" is Monsieur the Marquis, driving through worn-out country to his worn-out village. Near the fountain the Marquis recognizes a grizzled mender of roads who earlier had been gaping at his carriage. The Marquis has the little man brought forward. In a polite voice the mender of roads describes seeing a man—"white as a spectre, tall as a spectre"— hanging from the drag of the carriage (the drag was used to slow the vehicle as it went downhill). Angered at not being told of this sooner, the Marquis orders Gabelle, his postmaster and tax collector, to keep an eye on the mender of roads.

The Marquis next rejects a desperate petition from a peasant woman and drives on to his high-roofed château. There he awaits a visitor from England, a "Monsieur Charles."

NOTE: A Pun

Monsieur Gabelle's name contains a pun: the *gabelle* was the despised salt-tax, a leading cause of the Revolution. Again, notice how Dickens takes every opportunity to prepare you for the Revolution in 1789.

CHAPTER 9

It's important to understand the action of Chapter 9 in order to follow plot twists ahead. What happens is basically simple: Charles Darnay (by now we've guessed he's the Marquis' nephew) arrives at the château, a large stone building with carved faces decorating it. He and his uncle share an elegant dinner while renewing old hostilities. The Marquis argues that repression is the only lasting philosophy, and swears to uphold the honor of his family through cruelty. Charles deplores his family's past wickedness, and renounces France and the château, which will be his after the Marquis dies. The men part for the night.

Dawn arrives with a great commotion. Another "stone face" has been added to the many stone faces that already adorn the great house: the Marquis is dead, stabbed in the heart. A note is attached to the killer's knife: *"Drive him fast to his tomb. This, from* JACQUES."

A straightforward and electrifying series of events, but you might pay attention to several details for future reference.

Charles Darnay's father and the current Marquis were brothers—again, on instance of doubles. Darnay is certain that his father's time was a wicked one.

Darnay is bound by his mother's dying words to administer the family estate, and to do so mercifully. The death of his father had left Darnay and his uncle joint inheritors.

The Marquis asks Darnay if he knows any other French refugees in England, particularly "a Doctor with a daughter." "Yes," answers Darnay, and on the Marquis' face we see an evil smile.

The Marquis has fallen out of favor at court. If he were better connected, he might well attempt to imprison his nephew secretly with a *lettre de cachet*. You'll remember that the *lettre* is the same "little instrument of correction" that sent Dr. Manette to the Bastille. The Marquis seems quite familiar with its uses.

CHAPTER 10

A year has passed since the assassination of Charles Darnay's uncle. His great stone château seems, to Darnay, "the mere mist of a dream." Now employed successfully as a tutor of French language and literature, Darnay decides to tell Dr. Manette of his deep love for Lucie. Darnay asks one favor: that the doctor put in a good word for him, if, and only if, Lucie reveals she loves Darnay.

Noticeably shaken, Dr. Manette finally promises Lucie to Darnay only on the condition he is "essential to her perfect happiness." In a mysterious but significant speech, the doctor states that anything held against the man Lucie loves, "any fancies . . . any apprehensions," will be dissolved for her sake.

Darnay tries to reveal his true name and explain why he's in England. Dr. Manette stops him short, extracting the second of "Two Promises": Darnay swears not to tell his secrets until the morning he marries Lucie.

Arriving home from errands, Lucie hears a "low hammering sound" from her father's bedroom—the sound of shoemaking. The encounter with Charles Darnay has had the worst possible effect on Dr. Manette, throwing him into amnesia. Lucie is terribly worried, but by walking and talking with her father is able to restore his normal consciousness.

CHAPTERS 11 AND 12

In the midst of gathering momentum, these two chapters provide a pause. Do you know people who consider their friendship a valuable prize? Then perhaps you'll smile at Stryver's belief that his wish to marry Lucie does her great honor.

For readers familiar with most of Dickens' work, *A Tale of Two Cities* seems untypical. These readers cite the novel's rapid pace, lighter than usual detail, and sparing use of humor and dialogue as departures from Dickens' usual style. These two chapters, however, come closer to "traditional" Dickens. Their contribution to the plot is relatively small, and they depend on humorous dialogue (such as Stryver's sudden reversal at the end of Chapter 12).

Yet Stryver the man isn't especially humorous. Dickens describes him sharply, in terms of his size and obnoxious "shouldering" ability. Stryver is the new man, making social and financial strides in Victorian society; he's a "fellow of delicacy" in no one's eyes but his own.

CHAPTER 13

Stryver is out of town for the summer, and Sydney Carton's spirits have sunk to an all-time low.

One day in August he calls on Lucie Manette to reveal his secret: he loves her, but realizes she can never love him in return. Carton admits that Lucie's pity and understanding have had a good effect on him. Still he can never change his "self-wasting" ways.

Agitated and weeping, Lucie promises not to tell anyone of Carton's declaration, the "last confidence" of his life.

As he leaves, Carton foresees Lucie married and with a child. He swears he would do anything, even give his life, to keep a life Lucie loved beside her.

NOTE: Dickens' Sentimentality

Dickens has been accused of excessive sentimentality, especially when one of his young heroines is involved. Sydney Carton's address to Lucie Manette is a case in point: he praises her "pure and innocent breast," and exclaims, "God bless you for your sweet compassion!"

Dickens means us to take this chapter seriously. Faced with his intentions, you should decide whether the emotional fireworks help or hinder the novel. On one hand, you can accept Carton as a man of extremes—a self-destructive alcoholic—who can carry off extravagant speeches. On the other hand, his dramatics may impress you as a little overdone. You may also succumb to modern taste, and grow somewhat weary of Lucie's unchanging goodness.

CHAPTER 14

At last we're let in on Jerry Cruncher's secret profession. He unearths recently buried bodies and sells them to doctors for medical research.

Leaving their post outside Tellson's, Cruncher and son join a funeral procession. The crowd has turned out to jeer, for the dead man, Roger Cly, was an unpopular spy at the Old Bailey. (You met Cly at Darnay's trial—he was the faithless servant.) Cly has one proper mourner, who flees the growing mob. The uncontrolled crowd riots on to Cly's graveside, gradually dispersing. Observing that Cly was "a young 'un and a straight made 'un," Jerry Cruncher visits a surgeon on his way back to Tellson's.

That night Cruncher and two companions trudge to the graveyard, with young Jerry following secretly at a distance. Through young Jerry's fearful eyes we watch the men dig up Cly's grave and apply a large corkscrewlike device to the coffin. Young Jerry has seen enough; thoroughly terrified, he races home.

The next morning Cruncher is out of sorts. He beats his wife, accusing her of praying against his "honest trade." Cruncher has turned no profits on the night's "fishing expedition." (We're not told what he turned up until Book III.)

NOTE: A Mob Scene

A London mob escorts Roger Cly's coffin to its grave. Most of the participants have no idea what they're jeering and rioting; any excuse for breaking windows and looting taverns suffices. This mob is tame compared to those you'll meet in Paris, but the scene is a prelude to the unbridled violence to come.

CHAPTER 15

This is a dramatic chapter of murder and sworn revenge. The scene has shifted to Saint Antoine and the Defarge wine shop, where secret activity is in the air. Defarge arrives with a little mender of roads, introducing him to the shop patrons as "Jacques," the code word for a revolutionary sympathizer.

Defarge leads the little man up to the very garret that once housed Dr. Manette. There, before an audience of Jacques One, Two, and Three (the same men who earlier surveyed the doctor through chinks in the door), the little mender of roads vividly recounts the story of Gaspard. The killer of Monsieur the Marquis, Charles Darnay's uncle, has been put to death. Soldiers drove him to the prison on the crag, then hung him on a forty-foot gallows above the town fountain. Gaspard hangs there still, frightening away the people, and casting a shadow that seems to strike across the earth.

Defarge and his fellow Jacques confer. Defarge announces that "the château and all the race" are "registered, as doomed to destruction." The keeper of the register? None other than Madame Defarge, who knits a record of all those condemned to die for their crimes. Into Madame Defarge's register now go the descendants of the dead Marquis. Think of the implication: the only descendant you've met is Charles Darnay.

His duty carried out, the provincial mender of roads makes a day trip with the Defarges to the great royal palace at Versailles. The Defarges' purpose is political indoctrination. They teach the mender of roads to recognize the rich and powerful he'll one day destroy.

CHAPTER 16

A spy infiltrates the Defarges' wine shop. John Barsad is now working for the French monarchy. As Barsad enters, Madame Defarge pins a rose in her headdress, warning off the people of Saint Antoine. Barsad praises the house cognac, trying to sound out the Defarges on Gaspard's death. How has Saint Antoine reacted? Madame and Monsieur Defarge answer the spy's questions politely but coldly. All the while Madame is knitting the name Barsad into her register of the doomed.

Barsad does score one telling point. When he mentions that Lucie Manette is about to marry Charles Darnay, nephew of the murdered Marquis, Defarge starts noticeably.

After Barsad leaves, Defarge expresses surprise that Lucie is about to marry a man marked for death. He hopes destiny will keep Darnay out of France. For her part, Madame Defarge feels no sympathy. "Still Knitting" reveals her as stronger and more unshakable than ever, untiringly patient for her day of justice. At nightfall she moves among the women of Saint Antoine—each one knitting—spreading her "missionary" creed of vengefulness.

NOTE: Life of a "Saint"

Saint Antoine has come into its own as a personification, a character in the story. In the last chapter the arrival of Defarge and the mender of roads lights a "kind of fire in the breast" of the suburb; here, when Barsad leaves the wine shop, "the Saint took courage to lounge in."

The notion of a lifelike "saint" welds the citizens of Saint Antoine into one, a collective force. An appropriate effect, since these people will soon be acting as part of a single, unreasoning entity: a mob.

CHAPTERS 17 AND 18

The marriage between Lucie Manette and Charles Darnay has deep consequences for Dr. Manette.

The night before the wedding Dr. Manette seems reconciled to losing his daughter. Not that he's losing her entirely; she and Charles Darnay will be living in the Soho house. The doctor and Lucie sit beneath their old plane tree, where for the first time since Darnay's trial he talks of his imprisonment. Lucie is troubled, but her father assures her he's recalling his old captivity only as a way of "thanking God for my great happiness."

The actual wedding day brings a complete turnaround. As soon as the couple drive off on their honeymoon, Dr. Manette lapses into amnesia. He doggedly begins making shoes. Jarvis Lorry and Miss Pross try without success to bring him back around, and the ninth evening Lorry despairingly observes that the shoemaker's hands have never been so skillful.

NOTE:
Can we isolate what's causing the doctor's amnesia? Partly, separation from Lucie—ever since their meeting in Paris father and daughter have been constantly together. But our most telling clue to Dr. Manette's behavior is the closed-door meeting he held with Charles Darnay just before the wedding. Recall that Darnay promised to reveal his true name, and reason for living in England, on his wedding morn-

ing. There's a connection between Charles Darnay's family, and Dr. Manette's long period of darkness in the Bastille.

CHAPTER 19

On the tenth morning after Lucie's wedding, the doctor regains his memory. Jarvis Lorry awakes to find his patient normally dressed and reading, yet all is not normal. The doctor thinks that only a day has passed, and his hands, stained from shoemaking, trouble him. With the confidentiality and tact developed from his years as a "man of business," Lorry approaches the doctor about what should be done. Lorry is careful to refer to Dr. Manette in the third person. As you may remember, he used the same third-person tactic back in 1775, explaining the doctor's sudden "resurrection" to Lucie.

Believing his worst symptoms have been conquered, Dr. Manette reluctantly allows his shoemaker's bench to be destroyed. Lorry and Miss Pross wait until the doctor has left to join the honeymooners, then they hack the bench to pieces and burn it. Dickens' description of the process makes the faithful friends look like ritual murderers. Indeed, Miss Pross and Lorry almost feel like accomplices in crime.

With this sinister description of innocence that looks like guilt, Dickens may be telling us that it's often hard to tell reality and unreality apart. Things aren't what they seem. On the other hand, Dickens may simply be adding to the thickening atmosphere of impending violence.

CHAPTER 20

On a visit to the newlyweds, Sydney Carton takes Charles Darnay aside and asks two favors: that Darnay forget the night of his Old Bailey trial, when Carton was drunk and rude; and that Carton be allowed to come and go in the Darnay household.

Darnay agrees to both requests. Later he refers to Carton as "careless and reckless." This sparks an impassioned declaration from Lucie that Carton is capable of great things.

Whose assessment of Carton are we to accept? Dickens endorses Lucie's motive, if not her conclusion, when he echoes earlier praise for her "sweet compassion." As for Carton, the jury is still out—he's emerging as a complicated figure.

CHAPTER 21

The first half of the chapter, set in London, may remind you of the passage-of-time sequences in old movies: you can almost see the pages dropping off the calendar. Lucie establishes a calm, happy home for her husband, father, and daughter, little Lucie. A son dies—not tragically, but with a radiant smile. Sydney Carton drops in six times a year, and little Lucie establishes a "strange sympathy" with him. Stryver the lawyer marries a rich widow, and is rejected in attempts to have her three dull sons tutored by Darnay.

In all, Dickens advances the action about seven years, to an evening in mid-July 1789. Jarvis Lorry is visiting the Darnays, very concerned about unrest in Paris.

Notice that the echoing footsteps of II, 6—"Hundreds of People"—are back. In the first half of the chapter some are harmless, including the tread of Lucie's child. But as the chapter shifts orientation toward Paris, the footsteps grow menacing, and then "headlong, mad, and dangerous."

July 14, 1789: Saint Antoine and Paris rise in rebellion at last. Led by Defarge, thousands storm the Bastille, the hated symbol of government oppression. Seven dazed prisoners are released, seven officials' heads are paraded on pikes. One of the heads, belonging to the governor of the prison, has been hacked off by Madame Defarge.

In the tumult Defarge orders one old jailer to lead him and revenge-hungry Jacques Three to One Hundred and Five, North Tower, Dr. Manette's old cell. The wine keeper searches the cell thoroughly. We don't learn what, if anything, he discovers.

The running-water imagery Dickens introduced earlier has been expanded. The Bastille attackers are a "sea of black and threatening waters . . . whose forces were yet unknown." More water follows, as the endless waves of rioting Parisians spill into the next chapter.

NOTE: Revolution!

The taking of the Bastille on July 14, 1789 kicked off the long-simmering French Revolution. Conquering the hated fortress-prison was a heady victory for the people, and July 14, Bastille Day, remains a national holiday in France, the equivalent of our July 4.

Dickens' account of the battle, and of the massacre of old Foulon in the next chapter, owe much to Thomas Carlyle's description in *The French Revolution* (see Sources).

CHAPTER 22

The slaughter of old Foulon, a notorious oppressor of the masses, and of his son-in-law are depicted graphically.

NOTE:

What is Dickens' attitude toward the mob he so vividly creates? Consider several possibilities.

The "day's bad work" revolts him. Dickens characterizes Foulon as an old man, begging pathetically for his life. The Revolutionary women who désert their children and aged parents to snatch up weapons, are worse, even, than the men. The Vengeance (the complimentary name bestowed on the plump wife of a starved grocer) seems especially unsympathetic.

The mob enthralls Dickens. He writes vigorously because he's involved, and he puts himself in the place of the shrieking women and stern men. The mob is a projection of Dickens' dark side, his feelings of political and social powerlessness.

Dickens deplores the mob's action, yet he sympathizes with their plight. The chapter's final scenes paint a picture of wailing, hungry children waiting for their parents' return from the slaughter. The men and women do their meager shopping, as usual. There is human fellowship, and there are lovers who, with "such a world around them and before them, loved and hoped."

CHAPTER 23

The burning of the Marquis' great château—done by outsiders but supported by all the villagers—marks a shift in Dickens' imagery. The Revolutionary "sea" has changed to rising fire. As the château flares, molten lead and iron boil in the fountain's marble basin. The water has been consumed.

Notice how the fire obliterates all traces of Charles Darnay's dead uncle: a stone face that resembles his is obscured, "as if it were the face of the cruel Marquis, burning at the stake." The villagers believe that the stone faces on the château have changed twice. After the Marquis was stabbed, they were faces of pain; when Gaspard died, they bore "avenging looks." The obliteration of these stone faces marks the end of the Marquis' influence. In a way, the fire is his second death—it shows that the Marquis' soldiers and functionaries have finally lost their power to protect his interests.

Also notice Dickens' care, during this fiery night, to add plot details. He tells us that Gabelle, the chief functionary, has been collecting few taxes these days, and no rent at all. Even so, the angry villagers surround Gabelle's house, hoping for vengeance. The tax collector is fortunate to survive the night.

CHAPTER 24

August 1792. Three years have passed since the storming of the Bastille. France has overthrown its monarchy and many nobles—collectively referred to as "Monseigneur"—have fled the country. These emigrants gather regularly at Tellson's Bank in London to mourn their past glory and curse the new order in France. One day a letter arrives at the bank for "Monsieur heretofore the Marquis St. Evrémonde," that is, for Charles Darnay. St. Evrémonde is Darnay's true name. He confided it to Dr. Manette on his wedding morning, and to no one else.

The mysterious letter has come from Gabelle, the tax collector. Following Darnay's instructions, Gabelle had eased the burden on the villagers; he has been arrested nonetheless and sent to L'Abbaye prison in Paris, charged with the crime of working for an emigrant. At once, Darnay resolves to go to Gabelle's aid. If you found yourself in Darnay's place, would you make such a trip? Readers have taken three conflicting perspectives on Darnay's decision.

Darnay's return to strife-filled France is sheer foolishness, akin to jogging through a minefield. Darnay is so confident his good intentions will protect him that he doesn't check out the current situation in France, or consider that the people might feel hostile toward any aristocrat, even a reformed one.

Courage, duty, and pride combine to send Darnay back to his homeland. He has a duty to free Gabelle, and to dispose of his property once and for all. What's more, his pride is touched by the insults of Stryver and the collected emigrants at Tellson's. Finally, as a much younger man than Jarvis Lorry, who is about to journey to Paris for Tellson's, Darnay feels that he, too, should be brave enough to handle the French situation.

Darnay is a tool of fate. France is his destiny; he's drawn to the violence there as if to a lodestone rock, or magnet. Lucie's fantasy of thundering footsteps is about to be realized.

BOOK THE THIRD
CHAPTER 1

Darnay travels slowly across France with a government-imposed escort. On arriving in Paris, he's promptly arrested under the terms of a recent, antiemigrant decree. Darnay's guard, Ernest Defarge, recognizes him as Lucie's husband, but he resolutely withholds aid.

On the way to his cell in La Force prison, Darnay encounters a group of imprisoned aristocrats. Their refinement and good manners amid filth and squalor make them seem ghostlike: "the crowning unreality of his long unreal ride." Here, finally, is a touch of sympathy in Dickens' treatment of the French aristocracy, now on its way out. Dickens seems genuinely to mourn the passing of aristocratic beauty, stateliness, elegance, and wit. Yet do you see a change in his essential characterization of the ruling classes? In power or out, the aristocrats are a picture of unreality. They don't mesh with life's true conditions.

Placed in solitary confinement ("in secret"), Darnay paces off the measurements of his cell. His mind is full of disturbing thought fragments—about Lucie, Dr. Manette, and his recent strange journey.

NOTE: The Guillotine

France guillotined its first victim, a highwayman, in 1792, but similar killing devices had been used elsewhere since the late Middle Ages. Though named for a French doctor, J. I. Guillotin—who advocated their use on the grounds that death by guillotine was virtually painless—the early guillotines in France were actually built by a German.

Go forward a moment to Dickens' description of the guillotine at the end of III, 4: "It was the sign of the regeneration of the human race. It superseded the Cross." Here Dickens ironically invokes his theme of resurrection, while pointing out that the Revolutionaries strove to reduce the power of the church. One radical even introduced the worship of a Goddess of Reason. In due course, he was guillotined.

CHAPTER 2

Lucie and Dr. Manette follow Darnay to Paris. They burst in on a surprised Jarvis Lorry, who knows nothing of Darnay's presence or difficulties.

We're in the midst of the September Massacres (September 2–6, 1792) when over a thousand prisoners in Paris were slaughtered. The murderers sharpen their weapons in the courtyard of Tellson's Paris office, at a whirring grindstone. Try comparing these blood-soaked "ruffians" with the wine-soaked citizens in front of Defarge's wine shop 17 years ago. Don't the smears of blood resemble those earlier smears of wine? Dickens has set up a deliberate correspondence between blood and wine. It's one way he evokes the spirit of Revolution.

Lucie, little Lucie, and Miss Pross spend the long, bloody night with Jarvis Lorry, in his rooms above Tellsons' headquarters. Dr. Manette leaves with a cheering crowd. As a former Bastille prisoner, the doctor has automatic prestige and influence with the masses. He's confident that his authority will save Charles Darnay.

CHAPTER 3

In the morning Jarvis Lorry finds lodgings for Lucie and Miss Pross, leaving them Jerry Cruncher as a bodyguard. Dr. Manette doesn't return, but sends a note via Defarge that Darnay is safe. Dr. Manette, Defarge, his wife, and The Vengeance go together to deliver a second note to Lucie, from Darnay himself.

The Defarges and The Vengeance cast a figurative shadow over Lucie and her child. The description is an alert that the Defarge trio constitutes a threat. As you should be coming to expect, Dickens again divides his world into light and darkness. Lucie, "the golden thread," is falling into the power of her dark opposite, Madame Defarge.

CHAPTER 4

The personal fortunes of Dr. Manette and his family are contrasted with the increasing agitation in France. Though unable to free his son-in-law, the doctor displays unforeseen strength. His past sufferings, previously the source of his weakness, now guarantee his safety and give him endurance for supporting his dependents as violence sweeps the country. Dr. Manette becomes inspecting physician at three prisons, visiting Darnay weekly and becoming one of the best-known men in Paris. Any signs of past imprisonment that now cling to him are positive; he's "a Spirit moving among mortals."

NOTE: The Reign of Terror

This phase of the Revolution began in September 1793. In the course of power struggles between various factions, Marie Antoinette and thousands of others of high rank and low were executed. The "law of the Suspected," which Dickens mentions, allowed for the denunciation of a broad range of people. This law eventually brought down the extremists who framed it, ending the Terror.

The "strong man of Old Scripture" is Samson, the name of the chief executioner at the guillotine.

CHAPTER 5

The chapter's centerpiece is the wild Carmagnole, a street dance done to a popular tune of the same name. Pay attention to Dickens' treatment of the Carmagnole. If you've ever seen films or reenactments of war dances, you may pick up similarities.

Charles Darnay's imprisonment has stretched to 15 months. Each afternoon Lucie stands across from La Force, hoping her husband may catch a glimpse of her. A little wood-sawyer, whom we knew formerly as the little mender of roads, takes suspicious notice of Lucie's comings and goings. On a December afternoon, standing at her usual post, Lucie first spots the Carmagnole and is terrified.

NOTE:

Look closely at these dancers, "delivered over to all devilry," and again compare them with the innocents of years ago, dancing in the spilled wine at Defarge's shop. Dickens' use of mob action and violence has led readers to claim that his gore is laid on with a trowel. In their view the book is dominated by jolting tumbrils—the carts carrying victims to the guillotine—and dropping heads. As a result the French Revolution becomes a lunatic bloodbath. Its complex causes and far-reaching consequences never appear.

These doubting readers raise an interesting question. What does the Revolution mean to Dickens, and for his novel? Let's look at the different possibilities.

1. The events of 1789 and after provide a colorful historic canvas for a story of individual courage and redemption. According to this view, Sydney Carton's final sacrifice is more significant than its backdrop.

2. Writing about violence is Dickens' method for exorcising personal frustrations—he imagines himself participating in the slaughter.

3. Revolutionary events conveniently fit the larger theme of fate. As we know, Dickens drew many incidents from Thomas Carlyle's account (see Sources). Dickens also relied on Carlyle's philosophy that the French nobility was doomed to fall, given its excesses. In *A Tale of Two Cities* Dickens adapts Carlyle's determinism—or belief in prior causes—to fiction. "All things run their course," he comments, implying that upheaval can't be avoided.

4. History provides ample opportunities for moralizing. Dickens upbraids the nobility for their evil ways, perhaps more strongly than he does the mob.

Jump to Chapter 13 where the Terror is labeled a "moral disorder," and to Chapter 15 where Dickens delivers his ultimate moral message: "Crush humanity out of shape once more, . . . and it will twist itself into the same tortured forms." In other words, cruelty begets cruelty. There's the suggestion, too, that the aristocracy got what it deserved.

5. What better subject than a Revolution for preaching social change? Some readers have regarded *A Tale* as Dickens' manifesto for a new order in England. Others point out that it contains not one concrete suggestion for reform. Dickens advises that rulers and ruled behave morally, without necessarily changing the established order. This second argument seems to be supported by Miss Pross. She's an undeniably good woman, yet a loyal follower of the British monarchy.

CHAPTERS 6 AND 7

Darnay's day in court comes at last. He is freed by the Tribunal, thanks to Dr. Manette's efforts and prestige, and the testimony of Gabelle.

"I have saved him," announces Dr. Manette. Is this a judgment you should take as final? Look at these signs that Dickens is already undercutting Dr. Manette's—and Charles Darnay's—"triumph."

The people carry Darnay home in a "wild dreamlike procession." They are Darnay's supporters, but they don't seem like it to him. Darnay half-imagines he's in a tumbril headed for the guillotine.

Appearances aside, Darnay's cheering crowd is fickle. Darnay well knows that the same people, "carried by another current, would have rushed at him" and torn him to pieces.

In the next chapter Dickens' hints and Lucie Darnay's "heavy fears" are realized. Darnay is retaken the night of his release. A shocked Dr. Manette learns that Darnay's denouncers were the Defarges and "one other," to be revealed the next day.

NOTE: Police-State Psychology

Readers have remarked on Dickens' deep understanding of the atmosphere and mentality of a society ruled by fear. The night before Darnay's trial the jailer calls 23 names, yet only 20 prisoners respond. The missing three, dead, have already been forgotten. This is typical of a totalitarian society, in which the individual sheds his or her importance. Think of the mass graves that characterize modern "terrors"—those carried out by Nazis, or Latin-American death squads—and you have an idea of Dickens' meaning.

Many of Darnay's fellow prisoners have a secret attraction to death: "a wild infection of the wildly shaken public mind." This is an insight into the mentality of a prison or police-state, in which people have an irresistible urge to confess, to conform to the will of the state. (After Sydney Carton dies, you might want to return to this passage, applying it not to politics, but to his personal motives.)

CHAPTER 8

Several strands of the plot meet here. As you follow the coincidences, keep in mind that Dickens had no shame in using them. He felt that a well-drawn, unified atmosphere made coincidence appear logical, even likely.

Miss Pross encounters her long-lost brother, Solomon, in a Parisian wine shop.

Sydney Carton, revealed as Lorry's secret guest, steps from the shadows. He and Jerry Cruncher, both present at Darnay's Old Bailey trial 13 years before, identify Solomon Pross as John Barsad. Having overheard Barsad's conversation in the wine shop, Carton further places him as a "Sheep of the Prisons," a spy.

In a conference between Barsad, Lorry, Carton, and Cruncher, Carton suggests that Barsad has a co-spy in Paris, Roger Cly. Barsad protests that Cly is dead, but Cruncher backs Carton up. He claims, with an air of authority that Cly was never in his coffin at Saint Pancras-in-the-Fields. In Carton's words, Cly has "feigned death and come to life again," an ironic description that puts Cly in the category of "resurrected" characters along with Darnay and Dr. Manette.

CHAPTER 9

We've reached the night before Charles Darnay's second trial. Though Darnay is in peril, the story's emphasis is shifting to Sydney Carton. While preparing to save Charles Darnay, Carton readies himself to die. He makes a deal with Barsad to gain access to the prisoner, and he purchases some unnamed, potent drugs. Prophetically he tells Jarvis Lorry, ". . . my young way was never the way to age."

During an all-night tramp through the Paris streets, Carton recalls at three separate moments the words read over his father's grave: "I am the Resurrection and the Life. . . ."

Dickens closes the chapter with a four-star revelation: at Darnay's retrial, Defarge produces a paper he found five years ago in One Hundred and Five, North Tower. Dead silence falls on the court, as all wait to hear Dr. Manette's long-lost words.

Imagine you're one of the original readers of *A Tale of Two Cities*, making weekly trips to the newsstand for the latest installment. At this point in the story you're hooked. The novel's last few chapters are remarkably compressed, filled to bursting with emotion and events. They're true page-turners.

CHAPTER 10

The contents of Dr. Manette's journal are "the substance" of the shadow that periodically falls on him. We finally peer into the dark cloud of his imprisonment.

Dr. Manette's journal contains some of the most theatrical writing in the novel. The violated peasant girl shrieking, "My husband, my father, and my brother!" then counting to twelve, her dying brother's passionate curse—both episodes could be set with little alteration on stage.

Depending on your taste, the theatrics may or may not appeal to you, but try to appreciate Dickens' skill in tying up plot ends. You've learned why Charles Darnay, as a member of the St. Evrémonde family, threw his new father-in-law into amnesiac shock; you know the reason behind Darnay's promises to his mother to treat his peasants fairly.

In the uproar following the reading of the journal and the pronouncing of Darnay's death sentence, it's easy to forget that one secret remains: the identity of the young sister, the only surviving member of the ill-used peasant family.

CHAPTERS 11 AND 12

The chapter titles, "Dusk" and "Darkness," refer not only to the time of day, but to the apparently darkening situation.

Lorry, Lucie, and Darnay himself are sure the death sentence will be carried out. Lucie even faints away in the courtroom. (Many actions in the novel mirror previous ones: remember that Lucie has fainted before in a courtroom where Darnay was on trial.) Now, Carton kisses her, murmuring, "A life you love"—words from his earlier promise. Dr. Manette goes off alone, hoping to reverse the jury's decision. Then Carton is off, with the "settled step" of a man who knows what he's doing.

Notice that Carton has taken the role of calling the shots. Who is left to act besides Carton? Lucie is prostrated by grief, Lorry is old, Pross and Cruncher can't speak the language. In Chapter 12 Dr. Manette, the former bulwark, lapses into amnesia. Only Carton behaves forcefully, polishing his plan to "resurrect" Darnay.

A stop at the Defarge wine shop serves to make Carton's likeness to Darnay known. It's a precaution—Carton is planning for Darnay later to pass as himself. Pretending a poor command of French, Carton learns of Madame Defarge's intentions to denounce Lucie, her child, and Dr. Manette. Smiting her chest, Madame Defarge reveals that she is the one survivor of "that peasant family so injured by the two Evrémonde brothers." Thérèse Defarge's all-consuming purpose is vengeance. She's as unreasoning and destructive as natural phenomena. When her husband gingerly suggests moderation, she responds, "Tell the wind and the fire where to stop; not me!"

Carton has two more errands: a last meeting with John Barsad in the shadow of the prison wall, and a talk with Jarvis Lorry. He and Lorry are interrupted by the arrival of Dr. Manette, piteously crying for his shoemaker's bench. The doctor had drawn all his recent strength from his power to save Charles Darnay; now, with Darnay doomed, Dr. Manette is a defeated man.

Carton and Lorry make preparations for escape. To avoid denunciation from Madame Defarge—damning testimony to be supplied by the little woodcutter—Lucie, her father, her daughter, and Lorry must leave France at once. They're to meet Carton at two o'clock in Tellson's courtyard, and then flee. Carton gives the proper exit papers to Lorry for safekeeping; then he escorts the confused doctor back to Lucie's house. Looking up at her window, Carton bids farewell, a reminder of the great love he holds in his heart. Sydney Carton will never see Lucie again.

CHAPTER 13

Charles Darnay prepares for the death he believes is coming, his journey to "the boundless everlasting sea." Notice how Dickens' depiction of water has evolved. In the city and village fountains water flowed as a source of life. Later it overflowed, a symbol of the destructive mob. Now, for Darnay, water again means life, everlasting life.

In the letters he writes to loved ones, Darnay never thinks to include Carton. Now that you know Carton will save Darnay's life, what do you think of the omission? It's irony, used by Dickens to heighten his ending. Darnay is amazed at Carton's sudden appearance, two hours before his scheduled execution. Darnay notices a great change in Carton—"something bright and remarkable in his look"—and fears he's seeing an "apparition."

Have you ever had an intuition that something, good or bad, was about to happen to a friend or member of your family? Darnay's fear for Sydney Carton is intuitive. About to die, Carton is indeed on his way to the spirit world. Powered by "supernatural" strength and will, Carton orders Darnay to exchange clothes with him and copy a letter he dictates to Lucie: "If it had been otherwise . . . " (if, presumably, Carton had married Lucie), "I should but have had so much the more to answer for." By now Darnay's handwriting is trailing off: Carton has been inconspicuously drugging his double. Barsad comes to carry Darnay's unconscious form to his family and waiting carriage.

When the jailer calls Darnay, Carton responds in his place. Following the jailer to a large, dark room, he encounters a young seamstress who had been imprisoned with Darnay in La Force. Carton's heart softens toward the innocent girl, and he comforts her. The act adds another dimension of nobility to his sacrifice. The seamstress realizes Carton is dying for another man, and asks to hold his "brave hand."

NOTE: A Dramatic Escape

To show the narrow escape of Lucie and her party, Dickens shifts from third to first person: "*We* strike into the skirting mud"; "*we* are for getting out and running. . . ." The change of voice draws readers into the action. You almost feel right in the carriage. Only one leading character is excluded from the escaping coach and the fellowship implied by "we": Sydney Carton, the perpetual outsider.

CHAPTER 14

Fearing her husband may try to warn Dr. Manette, Madame Defarge plans to denounce Lucie and her father that very night.

Armed with concealed pistol and dagger, Madame Defarge sets off for Lucie's house. She hopes to catch her prey "in a state of mind to impeach the justice of the Republic." In effect, any mourning Lucie displayed for her husband would "impeach" the Republic's justice, and dig her own grave.

Dickens portrays Madame Defarge as a strong, fearless, attractive woman who's also a tigress. While deploring her heartlessness, Dickens seems fascinated by it. His reluctant admiration is evident when he says Madame's dark hair "looked rich under her coarse red cap." Her walk has "the supple freedom of a woman who has habitually walked . . . on the brown sea-sand." When you finish the novel think about Madame Defarge and Lucie Manette. Which character do you remember more vividly? For some readers, Madame Defarge stands out. Evil determination lends her enduring interest.

As Madame Defarge draws nearer, Miss Pross and Jerry Cruncher make their own preparations for escaping France. Cruncher repents of his sins—body snatching and wife beating—but Miss Pross is too preoccupied to understand him. She and Cruncher are to follow Lucie's party in a light carriage. For the sake of good strategy, Miss Pross arranges to meet Cruncher and their carriage at 3 o'clock at the cathedral door. He leaves—and Miss Pross faces Madame Defarge alone.

How might you characterize the struggle between these two strong women?

Love versus hatred: Miss Pross fights for her fiercely beloved "Ladybird"; Madame Defarge fights from her consuming hatred of the St. Evrémondes and their class.

Life versus death: Madame Defarge's unannounced entrance causes Miss Pross to drop a basin of water. The spilled water, a life-force, flows to meet Madame Defarge's feet, which have marched through "much staining blood." The meeting of water with blood signals the confrontation between life and death that follows.

Britain versus France: The two women are very determined, but direct opposites. Each believes the other's nationality to be a weakness. "You shall not get the better of me," announces Miss Pross. "I am an Englishwoman." Earlier in the story Miss Pross' self-proclaimed Britishness has comic overtones. Here it is deadly serious.

The struggle results in Madame Defarge's death by her own pistol. Miss Pross meets Jerry on schedule, and they make their escape. What is the price of Miss Pross' victory? She's rendered deaf forever. We're left to speculate on what her deafness means. For some readers, it's a sober statement of the realities of life: neither love nor patriotism can ever triumph completely.

CHAPTER 15

How do you respond to the death of Sydney Carton? Many readers find an undeniable sadness and impact. Carton's final journey in the rumbling death-cart is a kind of twist on the novel's opening journey where Jarvis Lorry recalled a man to life. Carton, too, has recalled someone to life—Charles Darnay—but at the cost of riding to his own death.

For the first time, Madame Defarge's chair at the guillotine is empty, and her knitting lies untouched. Madame Defarge's death has ensured the safe escape of the Darnay family and friends, but it cannot help Carton now. Just before he dies, making the ultimate sacrifice for Lucie, the words of the burial service pass once more through his mind: "I am the Resurrection and the Life. . . ." Sacrifice and resurrection: Carton's death interweaves these two great themes of the novel.

Let the power of Carton's act—and Dickens' skill in depicting it—sink in. Then, consider whether the novel's ending is truly hopeful, or if it has pessimistic overtones. The last few pages can be read from both points of view.

Chances are you've heard the novel's famous closing words, "It is a far, far better thing that I do, than I have ever done. . . ." These words end Sydney Carton's final prophetic vision in which all wrongs are set right. The vision is proof of a hopeful ending, proof that Carton doesn't die in vain. In it the current oppressors die on their own guillotine; a beautiful France rises out of the ashes; Dr. Manette recovers his sanity; and Lucie Darnay's son, named for Carton, becomes an honored man who brings his own child to see the place of Carton's sacrifice. Through the act of fulfilling his old promise to Lucie, Carton demonstrates that individual love can triumph over a chaotic society—and the march of history.

But note how Dickens qualifies Carton's vision with the word "if." *If* Carton's thoughts had been prophetic, they would have been the hopeful ones recorded.

Jump briefly to the beginning of the chapter. Compare Carton's "sublime prophetic face" as he steps up to the executioner with the tumbrils bringing the "day's wine" to the guillotine. Tumbrils and guillotine, Dickens tells us, are the inevitable result of humanity crushed "out of shape" by cruel rulers. The carts carrying the doomed are identical in underlying wickedness to "the carriages of absolute monarchs." Dickens labels the death-carts "changeless and hopeless," which seems to contradict Carton's glowing forecast of a beautiful France rising from the abyss.

How might you explain the apparent contradiction between the chapter's gloomy opening and Carton's glorious vision at the end? One school of readers holds that Dickens made his last pages hopeful in order to please his readers. Deep down he believed Carton's death more inevitable than glorious, just as he believed that history was determined or made inevitable by a society's actions.

A second group of readers charges Dickens with failing to achieve one of his aims—tying the destiny of individuals with the progress of history. A happy life for the Darnays, these readers argue, wouldn't guarantee a smooth road ahead for the French people.

As an independent reader, forming your own opinion on the novel's ending, you may find yourself accepting parts of all of the above views.

A STEP BEYOND

Tests and Answers

TESTS

Test 1

1. The novel is divided into three parts: ＿＿＿＿
   "Recalled to Life," "The Golden Thread,"
   and
   A. "Liberty, Equality, Fraternity"
   B. "The Track of the Storm"
   C. "The Substance of the Shadow"

2. Following "It was the best of times, it was the ＿＿＿＿
   worst of times," Dickens wrote,
   A. "It was the age of wisdom, it was the age of
   foolishness"
   B. "It was the dawn of liberty, the evening of
   repression"
   C. "It was a time to give thanks, a time to
   despair"

3. Jarvis Lorry's return message to Jerry ＿＿＿＿
   Cruncher was
   A. WAIT AT DOVER FOR MAM'SELLE
   B. BURIED HOW LONG?
   C. RECALLED TO LIFE

4. Dr. Alexandre Manette had been imprisoned ＿＿＿＿
   by
   A. a *lettre de cachet*
   B. a Star Chamber hearing
   C. a *raison d'être*

5. One of the recurring themes of the book is _____
   A. the purification of society during the Reign of Terror
   B. Mme. Defarge's spouting of revolutionary slogans
   C. Miss Pross' dedication to Lucie

6. An aspect of symbolism is seen in _____
   A. Lucie's golden hair
   B. the red wine flowing from the broken cask
   C. Jerry's activities as a grave robber

7. The Defarges kept the door to Dr. Manette's room locked because _____
   A. they felt he could not handle the idea of freedom
   B. they wished to protect him from the Jacquerie
   C. they were afraid he might wander off

8. In Chapter 4, Dickens uses a metaphor in which he compares a raging sea to _____
   A. the dangers of life in the 18th century
   B. the French Revolution
   C. the brutality of the aristocratic class

9. Charles Darnay's London trial gives Dickens the opportunity to _____
   A. explain the workings of the Old Bailey
   B. lash out at the English penal system
   C. describe the techniques for the bribing of judges

10. The jackal and the lion stand for _____
    A. Carton and Darnay
    B. Carton and Stryver
    C. Darnay and Barsad

11. Analyze Dickens' attitude toward the mob, giving examples from the novel.

12. Discuss the theme of fate in *A Tale of Two Cities*, relating it to history and to the lives of the characters.

13. Trace the evolution of water imagery in *A Tale of Two Cities*, citing three examples.

14. The coincidences in *A Tale of Two Cities* are piled so high as to be implausible. True or false? Support your position with evidence from the novel.

15. *A Tale of Two Cities* is a tale of symmetries. Many actions are balanced by previous ones. Discuss in detail one pair of symmetrical scenes, and explain their importance.

Test 2

1. In the early part of the novel, Carton's life is _____ described as one of
   A. "alcohol and reverie"
   B. "promise in shackles"
   C. "rust and repose"

2. The message on the knife that was used to _____ slay Monsieur the Marquis read
   A. "Drive him fast to his tomb"
   B. "Sic semper tyrannis"
   C. "May you rot in hell"

3. Dr. Manette's relapse came when he _____
   A. was taken back to the ancient prison
   B. learned of Darnay's parentage
   C. saw the pile of shoes

4. If Gabelle had been slain by the mob, _____
   A. the St. Evrémondes would have been deprived of their revenge

B. it would have enraged the Defarges

C. Darnay would not have been summoned back to France

5. The "one hideous figure" whose ominous _____ shadow dominated the bloody days of the Revolution was

A. The Vengeance

B. La Guillotine

C. Mme. Defarge

6. The Carmagnole was _____

A. the nickname for the "mender of roads"

B. the popular song of the Revolution

C. Mme. Defarge's knitting register

7. Jerry Cruncher contributes to the plot by _____

A. admitting that he was a Resurrection Man

B. revealing that Roger Cly had not been executed and buried

C. exposing Solomon Pross as John Barsad

8. Mme. Defarge's secret is that _____

A. her son had been run over by the cruel Marquis

B. her sister had been killed by Darnay's family

C. her father had been Dr. Manette's cellmate

9. A 70-year-old farmer-general and a young _____ seamstress

A. testified to the St. Evrémonde family's brutality

B. were to accompany Darnay to the guillotine

C. were part of the citizens' revolutionary tribunal

10. As a result of her confrontation with Mme. _____
Defarge, Miss Pross
    A. became permanently deafened
    B. secured the roster of doomed noblemen
    C. endangered the lives of Lucie and her little
       daughter

11. The novel's leading themes of resurrection and sacrifice
(renunciation) are intertwined. Discuss.

12. Sydney Carton's great sacrifice is, on the whole, a life-
affirming act. Support or refute, giving evidence from
the novel.

13. Dr. Manette's prison experience has good as well as bad
effects on his personality. Discuss.

14. Excluding Charles Darnay and Sydney Carton, give
three pairs of doubles in the novel and explain their
significance.

15. Compare the two cities, London and Paris, in this novel.

ANSWERS

Test 1

1. B   **2.** A   **3.** C   **4.** A   **5.** C   **6.** B
7. A   **8.** B   **9.** B   **10.** B

11. Dickens regards the mobs he creates with mixed
emotions. You may want to explore each side of his reaction. On a conscious level he sees the mob as a blind, unreasoning force, and disapproves. Subconsciously he's fascinated by mob violence.

Compare several different mobs in the novel: the Londoners who make a riot of Roger Cly's funeral procession;
the conquerors of the Bastille; the rioters of the bloody September massacres. What does Dickens show them doing?

What words does he use to describe them? Discuss what Dickens wants you to think about these mindless rioters.

Yet to carry out his political themes Dickens also sympathizes with the rioters' motives. Discuss how he fits these scenes of street violence into his political statements and his themes.

Finally, consider why Dickens gave such extended, vivid treatment to these mob scenes. Dickens writes vigorously about the mob perhaps because at a deep, unconscious level, he identifies with it. Discuss the effect of this dramatic intensity on your emotional reaction to the novel.

12.   Dickens introduces fate as early as the first chapter, personified as "The Woodman, Fate." Discuss how this figure prepares us for the bloody Revolution. What forces in history seem to be at work?

Now turn to discuss how individual characters are caught irretrievably in the web of events. For example, Lucie Manette hears echoes of hundreds of footsteps, which are fated to thunder into her life. Charles Darnay is drawn to France—and personal peril—as if pulled by a magnet. Look also at the Marquis St. Evrémonde, Madame Defarge, John Barsad. Finally, discuss how Dickens' larger patterns of structure—his use of coincidence and tightly interconnected subplots—express a sense that fate cannot be controlled.

13.   Begin by setting up certain things that water may stand for, such as a source of life, the unstoppable flow of fate, cleansing renewal, or the obliteration of death. Then devote one paragraph to each of three examples of water imagery.

For example, water appears in fountains—in the square of Saint Antoine, in the Marquis' impoverished village, and at his château. Look also at water running in rivers. Discuss how bodies of water appear in the book: you might want to compare what they seem to symbolize in two or three different stages of the story.

You might also look at places where Dickens brings in water imagery as a metaphor, to express the nature of something else. For example, the mob is compared to a rising, angry sea, a natural phenomenon gone berserk. Alone in his prison cell, Darnay prepares for his "journey to the boundless everlasting sea"; for Sydney Carton, dying in Darnay's stead, life flashes away "like one great heave of water." Here you will need to quote images directly from the novel, and discuss the passages in which they appear.

14. *True.* Discuss how the action of the novel turns on coincidences large and small, and compare this to the haphazard nature of real life. Do you feel manipulated by this, and if so, how does it affect your response to the novel in general? To support your view you should analyze a couple of coincidences that seem especially implausible to you. For example, Miss Pross runs into her long-lost brother, Solomon. Discuss this episode's dramatic effect and its relation to the plot.

False. Discuss how the novel's coincidences are plausible within the boundaries of the novel itself. First of all, analyze Dickens' thematic structure of parallels and contrasts, and his plot structure of closely interrelated characters. Are you surprised that these same characters turn up again and again? How do their reappearances further not only the plot, but also the novel's meaning?

Then zero in on a particular example of Dickens' closely crafted artistry. Ernest Defarge, for example, is a prototype of the Revolutionary leader: he's in the thick of all action related to the uprisings; his presence at Darnay's arrest may seem pat, but it is consistent with his role. As for John Barsad, quintessentially a spy, he fills in whenever a spy is needed.

How does Dickens prepare us for his coincidences? Look, for instance, at Miss Pross' brother—what do we know of him before he turns up? How does Dickens "plant" the coincidence of Roger Cly's connection with Barsad? Does this make the plot development seem more inevitable than coincidental? How do these events fit into the larger theme of fate?

15. Begin by discussing what the effect of paired scenes might be. Relate this briefly to other doubles in the novel, such as Carton and Darnay, or London and Paris. Then introduce the pair of scenes you will discuss. Here are some possible pairs.

The novel opens and closes with a fateful journey. In Book I, Chapter 2 Jarvis Lorry travels to recall Dr. Manette to life; in III, 15 Sydney Carton rides to his death. Lorry's journey introduced the prevailing theme of resurrection, while Carton's takes the theme to its culmination.

Lucie Manette twice faints in a courtroom where Charles Darnay is being tried; Sydney Carton twice sees to her comfort. Lucie's first fainting spell, in the Old Bailey, alerts us to her growing tenderness toward Darnay. Similarly, Carton's reaction tells us he's grown interested in her. In III, 12, after Darnay has been condemned to die, Carton carries out Darnay's wife's limp figure, showing his great love for Lucie—and his intention to lay down his life for her.

Carton twice saves Darnay from unjust execution, both times relying on their close physical resemblance. The outcome of Darnay's trial gives Carton the idea of substituting himself for Darnay at the end of the novel.

Whichever scenes you choose, analyze first one then the other in detail, placing them in the plot and relating them to the novel's themes.

Test 2

1. C	**2.** A	**3.** B	**4.** C	**5.** B	**6.** B
7. B	**8.** B	**9.** B	**10.** A		

11. One useful way to approach a question like this is to compare a series of characters whose actions exemplify the theme. Discuss the novel's three leading male characters—Dr. Manette, Charles Darnay, and Sydney Carton—in terms of how each acts out both resurrection and sacrifice.

Dr. Manette is "recalled to life" after 18 years' solitary imprisonment in the Bastille. How is he brought back fully into the stream of life? Then look at the sacrifices the doctor makes for Lucie, such as relinquishing her to the man she loves. How do Manette's breakdowns emphasize his sacrifices? How do these connect to his resurrection?

Charles Darnay has the honor of being "recalled to life" on three occasions, yet his sacrifices are what lead him into those deathly situations. Making frequent trips to France to carry out his mother's last wishes leaves him open to British charges of espionage, while renouncing his French property makes him a target of Revolutionary justice.

In Sydney Carton, renunciation and resurrection are most nearly joined. He renounces Lucie, and then dies for the man she loves. Carton's sacrifice resurrects Darnay to earthly existence, and assures Carton himself eternal life—a "far, far better rest" than he's ever known.

Finish by discussing how these characters' actions develop these themes in the novel as a whole. What is the importance of having these themes intertwined?

12. You can refute this statement by showing how Carton seems doomed to die. Discuss death imagery in the earliest descriptions of him; discuss how to react to his "wasted" life of drinking and subservience to Stryver. Finally, relate this to Carton's ending vision. Do you feel that by dying Carton has given into the force calling him all his life?

You can support this statement by showing that Carton's sacrifice is not only a better thing than he's ever done, but a more positive one. Analyze his mood and the appearance he makes in his dying scene. Discuss the value of his sacrifice to other characters, and then relate it to the novel as a whole: how does Carton's death resolve the novel's themes? Compare Carton's death to Christ's sacrifice, which redeemed all mankind.

13.   First discuss the bad effects of 18 years as a solitary Bastille prisoner on Dr. Manette. Analyze the emotional impact of the specific form his madness takes (the amnesia, the shoemaking). How permanent is the doctor's madness? Discuss its recurrences, and talk about your own reaction to them.

Then show the positive side of the doctor's experience. According to the Revolutionaries, his suffering is no mark of shame, but rather a mark of heroism and a source of power. Is this borne out? Look at the doctor's actions during the dark 15 months his son-in-law spends in La Force, and at his appearance in court on Darnay's behalf. What is your reaction to him there?

Conclude by discussing how Dr. Manette's imprisonment develops themes of the novel. Is the good or the bad effect of the Bastille most important overall?

14.   Discuss each pair in a paragraph. You may choose to look at one of these "twins," focusing on their similarities and their differences:

The St. Evrémonde brothers: Charles Darnay's father and uncle. Though Darnay's father has greater authority, the St. Evrémondes are spiritually indistinguishable—they're a double helping of evil.

Jerry Cruncher and son. A perfect miniature of his father—to the roots of his spiky hair—young Jerry represents the continuation of the family line. After his initial fright subsides, young Jerry even considers going into grave robbing, just like dad.

The little mender of roads/the wood-sawyer. One character, but in effect a split personality. As the little mender of roads he's a typical submissive peasant: the Revolution transforms him: the wood-sawyer is bloodthirsty and vindictive—again representative of the masses who, overnight, became a political force.

Madame Defarge and Miss Pross. Both women are strong, protective, and fiercely loyal. One is English, one French; one is good, the other evil.

15.   Your opening paragraph should explain why you're comparing London and Paris. In each paragraph after that, pick one feature and discuss it in relation to both cities. For example, you could compare their political climates; the types of characters who seem dominant in each place; how their mobs behave; how their courts operate; the kind of events in the plot that take place there (weddings, murders, births, etc.). In your final paragraph discuss how Dickens seems to feel about them both. Include a discussion of how he split the book's action between the two cities, and which you feel has the greater dramatic impact.

Term Paper Ideas

1.   Compare and contrast the doubles, Charles Darnay and Sydney Carton. In what sense do they form halves of a single personality? How are they individuals in their own right?

2.   Explore Lucie Manette's role in the novel. Include her influence on the plot, and her symbolic importance.

3. Madame Defarge: human being, or robot of vengeance? Support your answer, considering motivation and character traits.

4. Analyze minor characters who personify emotions and/or social classes. Include in your discussion The Vengeance, Monseigneur, and the little mender of roads/woodsawyer.

5. Discuss the following characters in terms of the habitual actions or occupations attributed to them: Stryver—"shouldering"; Madame Defarge—knitting; Jarvis Lorry—business. How do these actions illuminate the characters' respective personalities?

6. Liberty, Equality, Fraternity—or Death. Time and again Dickens repeats the Revolutionary slogan. How does the theme of death figure in the novel? Discuss its influence on the plot, the number and varieties of death, and Dickens' attitude toward the subject.

7. Examine the theme of prisons in *A Tale of Two Cities*. How do prisons affect the atmosphere and plot?

8. Dickens' themes of resurrection and sacrifice are closely joined. Discuss, with particular attention to the death of Sydney Carton.

9. At the end of the novel love conquers all. True or false? Support your answer with examples of loving characters—Lucie Manette, Sydney Carton, Miss Pross—giving their influence on the novel's outcome.

10. The world of *A Tale of Two Cities* is a world of lights and darks. Identify the forces of light and dark in the story (characters, institutions, natural phenomena), and discuss their contribution to the overall atmosphere.

11. Reality versus unreality: Dickens' characters often find it hard to distinguish between the two. List some of the images, characters, and incidents belonging to each state;

discuss which is preferable—reality or unreality—and why.

12. How does the novel's Christian imagery relate to its themes and plot? Discuss in terms of Carton's sacrifice, and Dickens' references to the "religion" of the guillotine.

13. Nearly every character in the novel has something to hide. Name the leading secrets, and explain their influence on the story's events.

14. Discuss Dickens' use of parallelism, citing three examples from the novel.

15. How is mirror imagery used in the story? List three mirrors in the novel, and relate them to character and theme development.

16. *A Tale of Two Cities* is weakest when theatric and melodramatic elements intrude. Support or refute, giving incidents from the story.

17. The novel was first published in brief, weekly installments. Trace the consequences of this format on Dickens' form and style.

18. The story is narrated almost entirely in the third person. Discuss the significance of the storyteller's occasional shifts to first person, citing two examples from the text.

19. Explore the symbolic connection between wine and blood, with special reference to the broken wine cask at the Defarges' shop.

Further Reading

CRITICAL WORKS

Essays on *A Tale of Two Cities*

Beckwith, Charles E., ed. *Twentieth Century Interpretations of A Tale of Two Cities.* Englewood Cliffs, N.J.: Prentice-Hall, 1972.

David, Earl. "Recalled to Life," in *The Flint and the Flame: The Artistry of Charles Dickens*. Columbia, Mo., 1963. pp. 238–54.

Fielding, K. J. "Separation—and *A Tale of Two Cities*," in *Charles Dickens: A Critical Introduction*, 2d ed. London: Longmans, 1965. pp. 189–206.

Johnson, Edgar. "The Tempest and the Ruined Garden," in *Charles Dickens: His Tragedy and Triumph*. New York: Simon & Schuster, 1952, vol. II. pp. 972–94.

Monod, Sylvère. "Some Stylistic Devices in *A Tale of Two Cities*," in *Dickens the Craftsman*. Carbondale, Ill., 1970. pp. 164–86.

Orwell, George. "Charles Dickens," in *The Collected Essays, Journalism and Letters of George Orwell*, ed. Sonia Orwell and Ian Angus. London: Penguin, 1972, vol. I. pp. 413–60.

Thurley, Geoffrey. "*A Tale of Two Cities*," in *The Dickens Myth: Its Genesis and Structure*. New York, 1976. pp. 255–75.

Dickens' Life and World

Avery, Gillian. *The Victorian People in Life and Literature*. New York, 1970.

Chesterton, G. K. *Charles Dickens: The Last of the Great Men*. New York: The Reader's Club, 1942.

Hardwick, Michael and Molly, comps. *The Charles Dickens Encyclopedia*. New York, 1973.

House, Humphrey. *The Dickens World*. New York: Oxford University Press, 1941.

Manowitz, Wolf. *Dickens of London*. London, 1976.

Wilson, Angus. *The World of Charles Dickens*. New York: Viking, 1970.

Wilson, Edmund. "Dickens: The Two Scrooges," in *The Wound and the Bow*. New York: Oxford University Press, 1947. pp. 1–109. Little direct commentary on *A Tale*, but fascinating psychological study of its author.

AUTHOR'S OTHER WORKS

Dickens' novels appeared initially in monthly or weekly installments. The years given below refer to first publication in book form.

The Pickwick Papers (1837)

Oliver Twist (1838)

Nicholas Nickleby (1839)

Master Humphrey's Clock (1840–41)

The Old Curiosity Shop (1841)

Martin Chuzzlewit (1844)

Dombey and Son (1848)

David Copperfield (1850)

Bleak House (1853)

Hard Times (1854)

Little Dorrit (1857)

Great Expectations (1861)

Our Mutual Friend (1865)

The Mystery of Edwin Drood (1870, uncompleted)

In addition to novels, Dickens wrote short stories, journalism, theater pieces, travel books, a history of England for children and, between 1843–48, a yearly Christmas story (the best known of these is *A Christmas Carol*, 1843).

Glossary

L'Abbaye Prison of the French monarchy, used by the Revolutionaries to jail aristocrats.

Barmecide Member of a fictional Persian family (in *The Arabian Nights*), who treated a beggar to a mock feast. Dickens' reference—"Barmecide room"—emphasizes that no dining ever occurred at Tellson's.

Bastille French fortress used to confine state prisoners; the Bastille was much hated by the people.

Bedlam Shortened form of Bethlehem Hospital for the Insane. In the 18th century visiting Bedlam was a popular

London excursion; in our own day the term has become
general for lunacy or chaos.

Conciergerie   Prison attached to the Palace of Justice in
Paris. Marie Antoinette, Robespierre, and other famous
prisoners of the Revolution awaited execution here;
between January 1793 and July 1794 nearly 2,600 prisoners left for the guillotine.

Convulsionists   Group of French religious enthusiasts giv-
en to wild dancing and fits; in fashion somewhat before
the time Dickens describes.

Fleet Street   London newspaper and business district, well
known to Dickens.

La Force   Old debtors' prison of Paris; during the Revolution it held political offenders.

Furies   In Greek and Roman mythology, minor deities
who relentlessly pursued sinners.

Gazette   Official government publication in England, con-
taining bankruptcy and other notices; to be "driven into
the Gazette" is to be published a bankrupt.

Gorgon's Head   Reference to Medusa, the Gorgon, a monster of Greek mythology. All who looked at Medusa were
turned to stone. The hero Perseus succeeded in cutting
off her head.

Hilary Term   Sitting of the English High Court of Justice,
extends from January to just before Easter.

Hôtel de Ville   French term for any city hall; here, the Paris
City Hall.

Jacquerie   Originally applied to a French peasant revolt in
the Middle Ages, the term came to mean any uprising of
the common people. *Jacques* was the old collective name
for French peasants, which Defarge and his revolutionary
friends co-opt, proudly, as a password: "How goes it,
Jacques?"

Leonora, Ballad of   Ballad of Gothic horror, composed in
1773 and popular among European romantics.

Michaelmas Term Fall sitting of English High Court of Justice, beginning after September 29 (the Feast of St. Michael).

Newgate Infamous London prison, now demolished; held prisoners awaiting trial at the Old Bailey, next door.

Old Bailey London court of law, remodeled into the Centre Criminal Court, but still widely called "Old Bailey."

Ranelagh Suburban pleasure garden popular with mid-18th-century Londoners, but falling out of favor when Stryver proposes inviting Lucie Manette there.

Saint Antoine Suburb (*faubourg*) of Paris that supported primitive manufacturing; its impoverished residents were the backbone of the Revolutionary mob.

Sardanapalus Greek name for king of ancient Assyria, made proverbial by his lavish display of wealth.

Sessions Periodic sittings or meetings of English justices of the peace; the Sessions deal with certain crimes and statutes.

Soho Cosmopolitan district of central London.

Temple Bar London gateway dividing Fleet Street from the Strand; the heads of executed traitors were displayed on it. Designed by Christopher Wren in 1670, Temple Bar was removed to a private estate in 1878.

Tower of London Fortress where those imprisoned for treason awaited trial.

Tuileries, Palace of Paris residence of the French kings, and hated symbol of the monarchy. Burnt down by French Revolutionaries of 1871.

Tyburn London gallows called "Tyburn tree," used until 1783 for hanging felons. Public executions became festivals, drawing large crowds.

Vauxhall Gardens Popular suburban resort, opened in 1660, closed in 1859—the year *A Tale of Two Cities* was printed.

Walton, Izaak Author of *The Compleat Angler*, 17th-century treatise on fishing.

Whitefriars London district between Thames and Fleet Street, long a haunt of fugitive debtors and criminals and so an appropriate address for Jerry Cruncher, body snatcher.

The Critics

On the Novel

A Tale of Two Cities . . . was a sacrifice of all his [Dickens'] greatest gifts; and in my opinion it shows that those gifts—of fantastic speech, of animistic description, of deeply absorbed symbolic overtones—are essential to the success of his action.

—*Angus Wilson*, The World of Charles Dickens, 1970

On the Revolution

The one thing that everyone who has read *A Tale of Two Cities* remembers is the Reign of Terror. The whole book is dominated by the guillotine— tumbrils thundering to and fro, bloody knives, heads bouncing into the basket, and sinister old women knitting as they watch.

. . . To this day, to the average Englishman, the French Revolution means no more than a pyramid of severed heads. It is a strange thing that Dickens, much more in sympathy with the ideas of the Revolution than most Englishmen of his time, should have played a part in creating this impression.

—*George Orwell*, "Charles Dickens," 1940

On the Characters

Of all the figures in the book Sydney Carton is the one who comes nearest to being deeply realized and the one with whom Dickens identified himself most closely.

> —*Edgar Johnson*, Charles Dickens,
> His Tragedy and Triumph, *1952*

Each of the three men grouped about Lucie Manette is "recalled to life." Her father regains his, on release from the Bastille; her husband's life is restored by his deliverance from La Force; and Carton finds his by seeking to lose it.

> —*K. J. Fielding, "Separation—and*
> A Tale of Two Cities," *1964*

Madame Defarge is the ultimate personification of the revolution in *A Tale of Two Cities*, and she is a being whom the uncontrolled desire for revenge has turned into a monster of pure evil. The final struggle between her and Miss Pross is a contest between the forces of hatred and of love.

> —*George Woodcock, Introduction to the*
> Penguin edition of A Tale of Two
> Cities, *1970*

If *A Tale of Two Cities* is the story of an innocent bourgeois doctor imprisoned by an unscrupulous elite, it is also the story of the responsible young aristocrat who disinherits himself out of disgust at his own class and tries to atone by a life of hard work. When we see Darnay as the representative of a class that needs to atone an historical culpability, he acquires new interest and depth.

> —*Geoffrey Thurley*, The Dickens
> Myth: Its Genesis and Structure,
> *1976*